A ROSE AMONGST THE WEEDS:
MY LIFE, MY WORDS

An autobiography and a family history

Christene Chadwick Moss
WITH Donald L Chadwick

Copyright © 2024 by Christene Chadwick Moss and Donald L Chadwick

ISBN: 978-1-7350965-8-2

All rights reserved. No part of this publication may be reproduced, distributed, or transmitted in any form or by any means, including photocopying, recording, or other electronic or mechanical, except in the case of brief quotations embodied in critical reviews and certain other non-commercial uses permitted by copyright law. For permission requests, write to the publisher, addressed "Attention permission Coordinator," at the following address.

Samone Publishing,
drsamone@samonepublishing.com

Unless otherwise noted, the photos herein are from the personal collection of Christene Chadwick Moss.

I dedicate this book to my husband, Franklin; my children, Edmond, Kimberlen, and Franklin Moss Jr. (wife, Mia Moss); my grandchildren, Kristen (husband, Aaron Sr.), Jorgette, Madeleine, Micah, and Franklin III; as well as my great-grandchildren, Aaron Jr., Ayra, and Ahri. Also, I dedicate this book to my parents and siblings, with a special dedication to my brother, Donald L Chadwick, and the Chadwick and Woods' families.

ACKNOWLEDGMENTS

I am grateful for my ancestors, who paved the way for my existence. They include my grandparents from my mother's side, Harry and Mossey Woods; my step-grandmother, Gentry Woods; my father's parents, Dock Chadwick and Laura Jane Matkins; and my parents, Dock Tucker Chadwick and Lula Mae Woods Chadwick.

Without God's touch, I couldn't have remembered the details of my childhood and life. Therefore, I am grateful for God's guidance throughout my life journey.

I owe a debt of gratitude to my family, especially my parents. My younger brothers, Donald L Chadwick and Alvin Chadwick, played a crucial role in raising my children and supporting me through high school and nursing school. Donald L, inspired me to write this book and provided the memories of our childhood and our father's stories of the Chadwick's history. His total support was essential for me to author this book.

Thank you to my wonderful children, Edmond, Kimberlen, and Franklin Jr. (Mia Moss), all my grandchildren, Kristen (Aaron Sr.), Jorgette, Madeleine, Micah, and Franklin III, and my great-grandchildren, Aaron Jr., Ayra, and Ahri. They listened, read, and gave input into my story. I also thank my friends and the community for participating in my journey.

Throughout the years, my late high school teacher and mentor, Mrs. Mary Grigsby, provided guidance and support. When I dropped out of school in the eleventh grade to have my baby, Mrs. Grigsby's words of encouragement kept me going. Later, when I returned to school, she inspired me to pursue my dreams of higher education. Throughout my career, Mrs. Grigsby supported me, even leading the charge to get a school named in my honor: Christene Chadwick Moss Elementary.

To Dr. Cherie Washington, I express my heartfelt gratitude for writing the foreword for my book. Your inspiring words and insights have added immense value to the book. You have eloquently captured the essence of my life on the school board, and your thoughtful words have genuinely resonated with me. I am honored to have your name associated with my work, and your support means the world to me.

Michelle Reynolds, I am grateful for your impressive writing skills and unwavering support throughout the project. You were my constant beta reader, offering feedback and asking thought-provoking questions that helped me complete it. Your steadfast belief in my ability to bring this book to fruition motivated me to continue and keep pushing forward.

I thank Anita Bunkley, my first editor, for helping me prepare my manuscript for publication, and my beta readers, Willie B. Jones and Dr. Gwendolyn Morrison, for reading my many pages and providing feedback for improvement.

To my dedicated group of educators and friends, I express my heartfelt thanks. Thank you for supporting me through the tough times on the school board and for being there for me when I needed your help. I appreciate all of you for having my back and helping me navigate obstacles that came my way. Special thanks to Rev. Dr. Michael Bell, Rev. Howard Mclean, Dr. Nancy Timmons, Jimmie Nealy, Keith Christmas, Patricia Williams, Dr. Cinto Ramos, Ricky Clark, Helen Williams, Cynthia Houston Brown, Sherry Breed, Gwen Carter, Edd Gray, Jackie Thompson, Cherie Washington, SaJade Miller, Walter Dansby, Nakia Cole, Dr. Carlos Walker, Helen Curtis, Gale Lewis, Janice Dilworth, and all the District 3 principals.

Dr. Monica Anderson, author, TED speaker, and podcast host, thank you for your constant encouragement as my Zeta Phi Beta Sorority-Inc. Psi Zeta Chapter Soror. Your words, "Keep pushing,

Soror; you will get there," and your book, *Launch Your Self-Publishing Journey*, have kept me on track.

Additionally, I am incredibly grateful to my siblings for recounting stories about our childhood during family gatherings with our parents. Every time we got together, my brothers told the same tales, and the family always had a good laugh. As a result, those stories became deeply ingrained in my memory.

To my nieces and nephews: Harold Davis, Carolyn Edwards Bullock, Stacy Chadwick Nickerson, Thomas Gene Chadwick, Bruce Chadwick Jr., Keith Chadwick, Kevin Chadwick, Courtney Chadwick, great niece, Michaella Titus-Terrell, Charles Myers, and Yolanda Chadwick Rollinson, thank you for the history, pictures, information, and dates you provided. Your input was critical.

Thanks to my cousin, Lee Johnson of Oklahoma, who kindly allowed me to use the Chadwick Family History.

Dr. Sheila Brown, publisher, thank you for insight and assistance throughout this time-consuming process of preparing a manuscript for publication.

Thank you Marvin D. Cloud, for the final editing and production of this body of work.

Finally, I thank my husband, Franklin Douglas Moss Sr., for reading my papers, recalling our history, advising me on travel stories, helping me edit my drafts, his unwavering support, and for being my rock for fifty years.

WHO IS CHRISTENE CHADWICK MOSS?

As I sit here writing, thinking about how to answer the question: "Who is Christene Chadwick Moss?" I hear a soft whisper in my ear. "Christene, can you really get in touch with whom you are?" Truth be told, we are now experiencing situations we have never seen in our lives. This has been a year like no other year! I never imagined I would live to see an international pandemic, the Coronavirus, an outbreak in the United States. In February 2020, the country was under lockdown. The advice given was to "stay home, wear a mask, wash your hands for 20 seconds, wear gloves, and practice social distancing."

As of 2022, there have been over one million deaths from COVID-19 in America. You could not have told me a few years ago that social media would be the main form of communication with my family and friends. Yet, "Zoom" has become our meeting place. I have been in more Zoom meetings than I care to draw attention to. God is still good, and the country is currently distributing not one, but two COVID-19 vaccines (since December 2020). We are now in the year 2024, and we have two variance boosters. Hopefully, God has finally gotten our attention as various germs surround us.

Now, let's address the previous question: Who is Christene Chadwick Moss? Let me start with my meager beginnings. I am a country girl whose family moved from a small rural town, Diana, Texas, to Lake Como, a small community in Fort Worth, Texas. I dropped out of high school because I had a baby. I married the same man twice and divorced him twice. Thank God for second chances. My family is my full-time support. I could not accomplish half of my endeavors without them. Many people don't understand that the duties of those who serve as elected officials, volunteers, and champions for the community, keep them away from their spouses, children, and loved ones. We sacrifice much time from our families to serve the communities we love and the constituents. It is a full-time job, no doubt about it. I know I could not serve without the support of my family.

I am married to former Fort Worth City Council Member Franklin Douglas Moss Sr. He is a Dunbar High School and Texas Wesleyan College graduate with a B.S. degree, and a graduate from The University of Texas with a M.S. degree. He is a historian and C.E.O. of Moss RED Group, Real Estate. We have three children. Our son, Edmond Lorance Moss, graduated from Richland High School and Memphis State University, where he pledged Phi Beta Sigma. He received his master's degree from Texas Wesleyan University. He is the staff accountant and property manager for the Phi Beta Sigma Fraternity, Inc., in Washington, D.C.

Our daughter, Kimberlen Camelia Moss Simpson, graduated from Dunbar High School and Austin College of Nursing. She retired with an honorable discharge from the Army. Kim also retired from her nursing career because of lupus. She lives in Little Elm, Texas.

Our youngest son, Franklin Douglas Moss Jr., graduated from Dunbar High School and Prairie View A.M. University, where he pledged Phi Beta Sigma. He currently serves as the C.E.O. of Franklin & Anthony Tailor/Clothier, (franklinandanthony.com.) in Fort Worth, Texas. Franklin & Anthony offers custom suits, shirts, and accessories. Franklin is co-founder and marketing director of Community Frontline, a non-profit brotherhood of men addressing the issues that cause suffering in our neighborhoods.

Our daughter-in-law, Mia Owens Moss, the wife of Franklin Jr., graduated from Southwest High School and attended the University of Texas at Arlington. She currently serves as the C.E.O. of Black Coffee, F.W., in Fort Worth, Texas. Mia opened Black Coffee F.W. near Texas Wesleyan University in the Polytechnic neighborhood, offering a variety of coffee drinks, baked goods, and snacks. She has expanded Black Coffee to the DFW Airport Terminal A.

We have three granddaughters: Kristen Monea Simpson Vance (Aaron) and Jorgette Louise Simpson, Kim's daughters; and Madeleine Marie Moss, Edmond's daughter. We also have two grandsons: Micah Shaun Mukoko and Franklin Douglas Moss III, (Franklin and Mia's sons) and three great-grandchildren: Aaron Vance Jr., Ayra Vance and Ahri Vance, born to Kristen and Aaron Sr.

My family, sitting left to right: Kimberlen Camelia Moss Simpson and me. Standing left to right are Franklin Moss Jr., Franklin Moss Sr., and Edmond Lorance Moss.

My first-born son, Edmond Lorance Moss, with his daughter, Madeleine Marie Moss and her mother, Jeanine Thomas Moss (Personal collection of Edmond Lorance Moss)

My daughter, Kimberlen Camelia Moss Simpson (left) with her daughters, Jorgette Louise Simpson and Kristen Monea Simpson Vance (Personal collection of Kimberlen Moss Simpson)

Left to right: Mia Owens Moss, middle son, Micah Shaun Mukoko, and last born son, Franklin Douglas Moss Jr. Out front is Franklin Douglas Moss III.

Granddaughter, Kristen Simpson Vance and husband, Arron Vance Sr. (Personal collection of Kristen Simpson Vance)

My great grandchildren left to right: Ahri, Ayra, and Aaron Vance Jr. (Personal collection of Kimberlen Simpson Moss)

Top: Daughter-in-law, Mia Owens Moss, CEO of Black Coffee F.W. Right: Son, Franklin Jr., CEO of Franklin & Anthony Clothier, suit by Franklin & Anthony. (Personal collection of Franklin Douglas Moss Jr.)

Contents

Who Is Christene Chadwick Moss?	ix
Foreword	xvii
Foreword	xix
Introduction	1

CHAPTER ONE

Humble Beginnings: My Childhood	9

CHAPTER TWO

Holland Quarters – Family Reunion Time	9

CHAPTER THREE

The Simple Life	19

CHAPTER FOUR

When Roots Become Wings	29

CHAPTER FIVE

Dock Tucker and Lula Mae Woods Chadwick	37

CHAPTER SIX

Entering Womanhood	59

CHAPTER SEVEN

Nursing is It	73

CHAPTER EIGHT

Husband Number Two	87

CHAPTER NINE

Family Matters 101

CHAPTER TEN

Life is Full of Surprises 111

CHAPTER ELEVEN

My Life in Politics 133

CHAPTER TWELVE

Bye, Bye Politics, Hello, Grandchildren 159

CHAPTER THIRTEEN

Finally 165

Lessons Learned From My Journey 169

The Accomplishments Of Christene Chadwick Moss   171

Christene Chadwick Moss: Through The Years   175

FOREWORD

Have you ever been in a crowded room and suddenly the atmosphere changes? I mean, you can feel an actual presence, a strong, impactful force that seems to overtake the room. That is the experience one has when Ms. Christene Chadwick Moss enters any room or event.

My name is Dr. Cherie Washington. I am an educator of 33 years and spent most of my executive leadership tenure in the Fort Worth Independent School District. That is where I met this dynamic leader. Ask anyone about her focus and one word comes to mind, "equity." For almost 30 years, Mrs. Moss served as a school board trustee. Persistently on the FWISD dais, these questions rang out, "What about the children of color?" "What are we doing to raise reading scores?" "How are we focusing on decreasing suspensions of our black boys?" "Are we treating our black students with respect?"

Her focus was not only on her students in District 3 but all students and employees in FWISD. She held a special place in her heart for nurses and new teachers. She celebrated them both and always asked, "What training or support are you providing to ensure these employees are successful?"

The message I remember most was when Ms. Moss spoke from the dias during a FWISD Board meeting regarding the death of George Floyd and Black Lives Matter. Here are a few remarks that still stick with me today:

"Today, regardless of your income status, if you are a middle-class black, from a black elite family, or have an educational background, if the system in place is unfair, it will treat you unfairly no matter who you are…. Also, we need to listen to our children who have become frustrated because they feel they do not have a voice. This interaction must be intentional and structured to reach all students, especially young men and boys of color."

—**Dr. Cherie Washington**

FOREWORD

When Chris, my sister, first mentioned the idea of writing her autobiography, my immediate thought was *how much my entire family could have benefited from it as a fundamental guide and model.* The name of that guide or model would have been: "When We Fall, We Get Up."

My family survived and coexisted with the current environment as usual. Mother always encouraged her offspring by saying, "Keep pressing forward!" Chris faced odds early in her teenage life; one in one hundred million. However, her achievements and accomplishments were astronomical because of two prevalent factors in her life: (1) God and (2) Powerful genes inherited from my mother, Lula Mae Woods Chadwick. Thanks, Mama!

This simple, yet powerful mantra, encapsulates resilience, determination, and the unwavering spirit to rise after adversity. Chris faced many challenges, setbacks, and unexpected turns in her life. However, her ability to stand up and keep pushing forward defined her upbringing. Whenever she faced a challenge, she became more assertive in her pursuit of success.

"When We Fall, We Get Up" reminds us that failure is not the end, but a sign that God is still shaping us. Chris, with her unyielding faith in God and the unwavering support of her family, believed that God would pave the way for her and her two children. Her journey is a testament to the strength that faith and family can provide in times of adversity.

This mantra encourages us to embrace our vulnerabilities, acknowledge our mistakes, and persevere with unwavering resolve. Whether facing a personal struggle, a family crisis, or a global challenge, it is a beacon of hope and resilience. When Chris stumbled by becoming a mother at 17 years old, getting married, and having a second child, life became complicated. The most devastating event for her was when her husband, who was in the armed forces, never returned home. She faced a crisis, but with God's help, she got up, dusted herself off, and asked God for the plan.

Chris has shared her journey and the lessons she learned through authoring her book, *The Rose Amongst the Weeds: My Life, My Words.*

I was fortunate enough to remember our family's history from my father's stories during my life with him, and that allowed us to recreate our childhood.

—Donald L Chadwick

INTRODUCTION

I am sharing a personal story titled, *The Rose Amongst the Weeds: My Life, My Words*. At 17, I became pregnant while in the eleventh grade, which led to a series of challenges. Looking back, I realize that the root cause of my problem was disobeying my mother's advice. She had warned me not to let boys into our house when no adult was present, but I ignored her. And, as a result, I faced the consequences of my actions.

I received a long sentence for what I did, but instead of pitying me, my mother encouraged me to be strong, learn to be a responsible mother, and complete my education. Despite the challenges, her unwavering support helped me become more independent. I learned a valuable lesson from my mistake and want young girls to understand that disobeying their parents' instructions can have negative consequences. It is essential to prioritize education over relationships and make better choices in life.

My journey involved marrying the same man twice and divorcing him twice because of infidelity. However, I did not give up. I picked up my two children, moved on, and never looked back. I worked hard to achieve my goals and entered politics, serving as a Fort Worth Independent School District Board Trustee for 29 years. With the support of many individuals, I developed relationships throughout my life, which made me a better person. Today, an elementary school and a children's library stand in my honor.

My message is one of determination and perseverance. No matter how difficult life may seem, giving up is never an option. We must keep moving forward with determination and effort, and success will eventually come our way.

Why am I sharing this book? Becoming a more seasoned adult brings about body changes. God has blessed me with a good portion of health and strength. I want my children, grandchildren, great-grandchildren, other family members, friends and acquaintances, to know me, not just from "whence" I have come! They should know about my ups and downs, my struggles and my challenges, and realize they are not simply in good company, but know that my aim is to inspire them. Look at my past accomplishments and think: *If she can push through, so can I! Anything worth having is worth pursuing. Do not expect anything for free. The Lord is not going to put on us more than we can bear.*

"I can do all things through Christ who strengthens me"
(Philippians 4:13).

Yes, this is the life I have lived, mistakes and all; it is the only life I have known. Therefore, it has been good to me and for me. I thank God, and I thank my family for loving me as I've loved them.

If the question arises, "What is the purpose of this writing?" I now have the time to visit my doctor's office and write. My bronchiectasis only occurs two or three times a week if I take my daily breathing treatments. The neuropathy in my toes is painful only when my toes are edematous and I wear shoes that are too small. Lastly, the weather plays a significant role in the arthritis in my knees, arms, back, legs, and other joints. Maybe, you see how blessed I am. I pray God continues to shower me with His grace. I will keep moving forward.

Keep pressing forward!

CHAPTER ONE

Humble Beginnings – My Childhood

While growing up in Lake Como, which is in west Fort Worth, I never knew what being poor looked like. Everyone in my neighborhood seemed to be in the same financial situation. What need was there to discuss it? Our teachers always encouraged us to study and do our best and they never made us feel like our community lacked anything. Looking back, I realize how lucky I was to have grown up in such a tight-knit community. Even though our neighborhood was black, I never felt like that was a disadvantage. I loved knowing all my neighbors and feeling like we were all a part of one big family.

Not much comes to mind when I think back to my early childhood in Diana, Texas. As a matter of fact, I contacted an old classmate from my first-grade class at Mount Enterprise School, Jean Elbert Crow, to see if she could help jog my memory. However, all she could recall was making mud pies, going to school, wearing our hair in long pigtails, and donning cotton sack dresses. Cotton sack dresses were popular back then. I remember people commenting on how cute I was and asking if Lula was my mother. Strangely enough, according to Jean, my family had already moved away when she attempted to contact me.

I was born in Diana, Texas, to Dock Tucker Chadwick and Lula Mae Woods Chadwick on February 11, 1943. I was the ninth of 12 children (eight boys and four girls). Diana is a small rural town in the northeastern corner of Texas, near Farm Road 726 and U.S. Highway 259. It's situated 12 miles east of Gilmer in eastern Upshur County. If you travel southeast, the distance from Diana to Carthage is 45.19 miles; if you travel north to Marshall, it's 27.9 miles. Diana was first settled in the early 1850s. The population was around 3000 residents in the 1950s. (Wikipediaorg)

We called my mother, "Mama" and we called my father, (Deddy). Mama named me Christene after her sister. My family and others called me and Aunt Christine, Chris. I have three younger brothers. My two older sisters, Aldotsie Chadwick Davis and Mary Virginia Chadwick Edwards, married and moved to Dallas, Texas, by the time I was five years old. My brother, Frank Thomas Chadwick, moved from Diana, Texas, to Houston, Texas, to live with our mother's sister, Christine Woods Bradford. My brother, Dock Tucker Chadwick Jr. died of pneumonia at the age of one. Aldotsie, Frank Thomas, Mary Virginia, Dock Tucker Jr., Mossey Neloise, Edward Thomas, and Howard were born in Carthage, Texas.

After Howard's birth, Deddy moved us to James, Texas, (later named, Diana). Adolphus (12/21/1940), Bruce (12/12/1944), Alvin (8/12/1946), and I (2/11/1943) were born in Diana, Texas. We lived in three locations. Our first home was on Walter Brazil's place, where Adolphus was born. My parents were sharecroppers. Our second home was on Highway 154 on Emmett Kingston's place, where Bruce, Alvin, and I were born. Donald L (10/14/1948) was born on the new place where Deddy built the two-room house on 10 acres of land. We lived across the street from Macedonia Apostolic Church, and I attended Mt. Enterprise School. Jean Crow was my classmate; her father was a school teacher.

Country Conflict – The Move

In November 1949, my father sold most of his inheritance–50 acres of land he received from his father–to support his eleven children. He sold a portion of his land, his home, cattle, and hogs to his brother and used the money to purchase land in Fort Worth. Upon acquiring the new land, my parents instructed their eight children to pack our belongings because we would soon move to Fort Worth. We lived in the country without streetlights, and it was dark from sundown to sunrise. To this day, the road remains without lights.

We were glad when our parents moved to the city. My parents loaded up our dog, Old Lee, my siblings and me, and we headed toward Fort Worth, Texas. At age six, I was unsure if I was happy or sad about leaving the country. I *was* glad to leave the darkness behind. It took Deddy a long time to drive to our new home. I thought the road would continue winding, as it led to Fort Worth. The tall, lush trees on either side of the road seemed to bid us farewell as we zoomed past them. I sat comfortably on my brother's lap, taking in the breathtaking view outside the window. My parents and little brother, Donald L, sat in the front seat while we squeezed into the back. Mossey, Adolphus, and Bruce sat in the back seat.

Alvin and I sat on their laps. It was a tight squeeze. By the time we arrived, my butt was sore. My brothers repeatedly said, "Chris, move over to the your other brother's lap." Riding was like musical chairs, from one lap to the other. Deddy stopped once and allowed us to stretch our legs. His best friend, our cousin, George Eddie, moved our belongings via Farmsville in his big truck. Edward Thomas and Howard rode in the back with the furniture. It excited us to reach our destination and embark on countless adventures.

The Move to Fort Worth – Lake Como

When we arrived in Fort Worth in November 1949, we lived in a rented house at 5206 Libby Street in Lake Como for a little over one year. The rented house was nothing like the country, which was surrounded by trees, land, cattle, horses, and chickens. There were streetlights, stores, houses nearby, and many new city shenanigans. There were other children in the nearby homes. This was unlike the country, where houses were not close together; we had to walk a distance to see our neighbors.

Lake Como is a neighborhood in west Fort Worth, made up of black families. It was separated from the white neighborhood by a barbed wire fence and a brick wall. In the 1940s, somebody built a brick wall topped with barbed wire that spanned about ten blocks to divide the predominantly black Como residents from their white neighbors in Ridglea. Signs on the Como side warned passers-by not to trespass.

The six-foot-tall chain-link fence ran north-south along the west side of Bryant Irvin Road. This barbed wire fence created a minor problem for anyone living in Lake Como and going to work at Ridglea Country Club. Bryant Irvin Road separated the Ridglea and Como neighborhoods. The "Ridglea Wall" kept Como residents out of Ridglea's retail district and, for some, created a long-distance trek between their homes and their jobs. The blacks in Lake Como worked as help for the whites in Ridglea. Many whites had built service quarters in their backyards for the blacks to live in and take care of their children.

My parents enrolled Mossey in I.M. Terrell High School, an all-black school across town on Baptist Hill. She rode the school bus every day to and from school. If she missed her bus, she had to ride the city bus to school. Terrell High School was the only high school in the city for black students in the 10th through 12th grade. After she enrolled, Mossey landed a job at the Como NewsStand. Mama enrolled E.T., Howard, Adolphus, and me into the Como school in our neighborhood. The Fort Worth school system enrolled us in a grade lower because we started school in the country when we were four. We attended school every day.

My mother taught us how to read before entering first grade. I can hear her now; "Dick, see Jane run, Run, Jane run." Those old books Mama got from the white families she worked for helped create my interest in reading. Later, she enrolled Bruce in

Our Mother of Vickery Catholic School, a private kindergarten school on Bonnell Street. In 1950, tuition cost $50.00 a month. When the new Como Elementary was ready to enroll students, my mother transferred Bruce to first grade at Como after a year at the Catholic school. Alvin and Donald L attended daycare in the Como Community Center near Boozies (cafe, club, etc.) until they were old enough for Como Elementary.

Living in Como was a unique experience. The community had a strong sense of pride in their identity. Black citizens purchased land and built their homes, surrounded by luxury and wealth. Years later, the Fourth of July Como parade would become the year's highlight for my children and me. The residents organized the largest parade in Fort Worth. As an elected official and growing up in Lake Como, I returned yearly and drove my car in the parade. My grandchildren loved throwing candy to the children and watching the floats and vehicles. Nothing in Fort Worth could compare to the Como Parade.

My grandchildren: Madeleine, Micah, and me, at the annual Fourth of July Lake Como parade.

CHAPTER TWO

Holland Quarters – Family Reunion Time

Traveling to our annual family reunions at Holland Quarters allowed the families to visit their loved ones buried in the Pine Grove Cemetery. The Holland Quarters Church (Pine Grove Baptist Church) is directly across from the cemetery. Burials in the cemetery were free, mostly because, after slavery, the Dock Tucker Chadwick family donated the land to Holland Quarters. The families that moved away continued to pay the groundskeeper for the annual grooming of the cemetery. My parents' burial plots are located there. To this day, Donald L reimburses the groundskeeper yearly for providing perpetual care to the Dock Tucker Chadwick family plots.

Our family traveled to Carthage, Texas, to Holland Quarters Pine Grove Baptist Church grounds at least once each August for family reunions. On the first Sunday in August, we gathered at the Pine Grove Baptist Church. On the third Sunday, we went to Diana, Texas, to the Macedonia Apostolic Church. E. T. and Mossey stayed home to work. Traveling to Carthage took my family all day. Today, it only takes two and a half hours. Our parents packed all the children in the car with the trunk filled with home-cooked food. Deddy, Mama, and all the others piled in the back seat, even if we had to sit in each other's laps. Mama would say, "Kids, get in the back."

The adults and children walked around on the church grounds in the blistering sun, eating food from all the car trunks. One could see the car trunks raised across the church grounds with all that delicious food inside.

After church service, dinner was served on the grounds. I could smell the aroma of chicken and dressing coming from the cars. It was as if the food called my name, and beckoned me to come over and indulge in the mouth-watering dishes. My aunt's car was always my first stop, and I never missed a chance to savor her food. No one cooked like my aunt; her food was simply the best. As I walked around the church grounds, I noticed every vehicle had various covered dishes, including fried chicken, green beans, mac and cheese, corn, field peas, pinto beans, greens, and fresh vegetables from their gardens.

Once I told my brothers, "Let's not eat the food our mother cooked at home; let's go to the other cars and eat." Unfortunately, when my mother heard about our food escapades, we could hear her across the church grounds as she yelled, "Chris, Bruce Harold, Alvin and Donald L, get back here!" We ran back to our car. It was always the hottest day in August. The sweat ran down our faces, and the adults had towels around their necks to wipe their foreheads and not allow their perspiration to fall into the food.

The women at the church, who were seasoned bakers, created the tallest and most delicious four-to-five-layer cakes I had ever seen. Baking was an essential part of women's lives back then, and the cakes were flavorful and would melt in your mouth. You had to grab a slice early, or they would all disappear by mid-afternoon. The cakes came in only a few flavors, including chocolate, which was rich; coconut with the accompanying fragrant aroma; lemon, which filled the air with its irresistible scent; and pound cakes that were silky-smooth and moist. They even made a pineapple upside-down cake with real pineapples on top. The only cake I did not like was angel food cake. It was too soft. Back in the day, the women didn't have electric mixers, but they could conjure up the most incredible cakes with their hands, made with love and care. My mother's cakes were always five or six layers and finishing one slice took an entire evening. Nowadays, we have numerous cake flavors made with the help of electric mixers.

When it came to pie, my mother was the only one who could bake one to my satisfaction. I always made sure to come back to our car for her sweet potato pie. Everyone would come to our car for my mother's food because she had a reputation for being a great soul food chef.

People would say, "Your mother's food melts in my mouth."

My reply was always, "Mother cooks that way at home every day."

The cafes and stores buzzed with activity at night. The place was alive with lights, loud music, card games, dominoes, and abundant food and drink. The children played hide and seek behind the trees while the adults danced and enjoyed their alcoholic beverages. I once asked my mother how did the food stay fresh all day without spoiling? She explained she made everything from scratch and without any preservatives. Later that night, we spent the night with our relatives, and the roads and houses were so dark that we could not even see ourselves. The next day, we returned home after a fun-filled night. That last night at Holland Quarters went down as always: A night to remember!

I always encourage my family to continue to host the Dock Tucker & Lula Mae Woods Chadwick reunion every two years. These gatherings are about getting to know our people and building strong relationships with family members. The bonds we form during these reunions are invaluable and contribute significantly to our sense of belonging and appreciation for our family.

Robert Myers of Houston, Texas, plans the Dock Tucker & Lula Mae Woods Chadwick family reunion every two years with the assistance of Younda Chadwick Rollinson of Denton, Texas, Kimberlen Moss Simpson of Little Elm, Texas, and Stacy Chadwick Nickerson of Arlington, Texas.

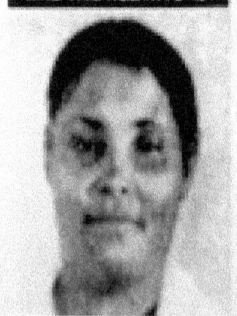

Carthage, Texas, July 1993. The Chadwick family continues to hold their reunions in East Texas.

Growing Up In Lake Como

I prepared my lunch every day and walked to school. My friend, Len Etter Howard, was smaller than me and a grade lower. That did not matter. We were neighborhood friends. She was an only child who lived with her mother directly across the street. Mrs. Howard was a soft-spoken lady who always smiled with a huge grin. She welcomed me into her home. Len's father did not live with them. I met him when he visited; he had bowlegs, was short, and wobbled when he walked.

When I was ready for school, I went to the edge of the road and called, "Len Etter, are you ready?"

She would always be prepared and answer, "Here I come!"

We walked to school together daily, rain, shine, sleet, or snow, from the 5100 block of Humbert to the school in the 5900 block of Libby. About halfway to the school, on Libby Street, lived the Martin family with two bad boys. The two boys threw rocks at us every day. We tried to tip-toe past their house. However, they always waited on us with stones in their hands.

As we neared their house, Len Etter would scream, "Chris, there are those bad boys!"

"Run, Len Etter!" I would say. We took off running toward the schoolhouse.

One day, a rock hit my books and frightened me. I yelled and told the boys, "I will tell my brother on you!"

However, they said, "We don't care; tell your brother."

After running away from the boys every day, I finally told Adolphus about them hurling the rocks. The boys left us alone after Adolphus followed us to school one day. He told them, "If you throw another rock at my sisters, I will come and beat you with the rocks." They never threw another one in our direction. We lived through all of that and grew up without bodily harm.

During my third-grade year, two girls, Earnestine Smith and Windell Lou Hall became rivals. Both girls were the only child in their families. Their mothers dressed them in pretty dresses, matching shoes, socks, ribbons, and purses every day. Earnestine was more popular and thought she was superior to Windell Lou. She would tell other girls not to play with Windell Lou or her friends, including Charlene McLane, Barbara Curley, and me.

However, I did not mind being friends with all the girls and enjoyed the company of my friends because of our positive attitudes toward each other. I did not care about how they dressed either; I believed for me, learning my lessons was more important than my attire. I wore dresses made of flour sack material because my mother used to buy flour in 20-pound cotton flower-design bags. After she cooked with the flour, she cut the sack into a pattern and made me a beautiful flower dress. Looking back, I realize I thought having fancy clothes was the key to feeling beautiful, but I felt just as pretty in my humble flour-sack dress.

My school friends and I performed all of our school activities together until the ninth grade, including playing basketball and

From the left, I am celebrating a with celebrating at Windell Lou's birthday party with Charlene McLane Adams, Barbara Curly Mitchell, and Windell Lou Hall Elzy. Friends since third grade, friends for life.

volleyball, taking P.E., and eating lunch. The teachers often said, "There go the four musketeers."

Charlene and Windell left Como in the tenth grade and graduated from I.M. Terrell High School.

After graduating, we reunited and were best friends for a long time. Charlene always called and said, "Let's go eat and see a movie on Saturday." We all had fun talking and laughing about our high school days. We took part in an activity every four to five months. I always invited them to the Sojourner Truth Theater downtown, and we attended musicals. Sadly, Charlene and Windell have passed away, but Barbara and I still celebrate our birthdays and talk on the telephone. We no longer attend the movies as often as we once did when it was the four of us.

In 1951, I was eight years old when my dad had our three-room home built at 5100 Humbert Street. He had purchased the land before we moved to Fort Worth. Lord, God, what a blessing! We lived at the corner of Humbert and Neville Streets. At that time, there were no houses on our side of the road to the west of us.

My parents, Dock Tucker and Lula Mae Woods Chadwick built our home at 5100 Humbert in Lake Como and it still stands.

Originally, we didn't have a sewer line extended to our property. The sewer line stopped about a block to the west of our land at Humbert and Merrick Street. We had more space in our new home and land to play games. Our home was the last house on the north side of the street.

At the beginning of the block to the west, there was a pond we had to cross to get to the next block. Our cousins, Edd and Mary Gray, and their children, Billy, Geneva, Dolma Jean, Dean, Bernard, Jeanelle, Edd Gray Jr., and other families lived in the next block. We called the pond, "the crawfish pond." We caught crawfish by using bacon for bait. After we caught them, we cleaned, cooked, and ate them.

The children of our cousin, Edd Gray Sr. and Mary Gray. Front row: Bernard, John, Edd Jr. Back row: Billy, Buna, Edd Sr., Mary, Dean, Gennell and Dolma Jean.

We lived across the street from Mr. Howard and Dorothy Strain and their children. Behind the Strains, the road dropped off into land that was full of trees. The land beyond the hill had dense trees, that obstructed our view beyond the treetops. When we stood on the hill, we could see West Victory Road and Texas Christian University's (TCU) stadium lights. No one could imagine what was under that hill. Little did we know that two families, the Fox sisters, lived under the hill. The Fox sisters lived in that wooded area.

Alvin and I were afraid to go under the hill, but we were curious about our new neighbors. Mama always said, "You are too nosey for your own good."

One day, we visited Mrs. Willie and her sister, Doll; the Fox sisters. While sitting in their kitchen, I pointed at the refrigerator and said to Alvin, "Look, what is that strange-looking animal coming out of the hole behind the refrigerator?" When Alvin saw the large animal, he freaked out.

He screamed, "Chris, let's get out of here and back up the hill!" He took off running up the hill.

I trailed him and hollered," Alvin, wait for me!"

When we got home, we told our father about the giant animal that resembled a cat that emerged from behind the refrigerator.

He laughed and said, "You saw one of the giant wood rats that live under the hill." Despite our initial fear, we continued to explore the area with our other siblings.

Growing up on Humbert Street with six brothers and an older sister was no joke. Our toilet was in an outhouse about 50 feet along the trail behind our house. Back then, one cherished paper of any kind to take to the toilet. We could crumble the paper to make it soft enough to wipe. For a girl, it was more difficult than for the boys. I hated the outhouse.

When I first started on my monthly cycle, I did not know what was happening. I told Mama I was bleeding when I went to the toilet. I would have appreciated what my mother said to me about starting my period if she had shared the information before it happened. The surprise of nature would have been a welcome experience. Instead, it made me run down the back trail from the outhouse, screaming like a wild child, "I am bleeding! I am bleeding!" Everyone knew what was happening but me. With the number of people in the house, you had certain times to go to the toilet. God, it was awful if Mama had to give you castor oil for a stomachache or a cold; you would "shit" for hours.

CHAPTER THREE

The Simple Life

One of my neatest experiences was watching my mother wash our clothes. Deddy attached cords to the trees in the backyard, to make a clothesline to dry our clothes. A large black iron pot in our backyard rested on an iron stand. My brothers filled the pot with water and built a fire underneath for Mama to wash our clothes. She washed the white clothes separately from the dark ones and she used a wash board to rub the clothes clean. An experience occurred when Mama poured bluing in the rinse water of the white garments. The water turned royal blue, but the clothes came out lily white. Observing the clothes-washing process brought excitement to my eyes. The siblings hung the dresses on a clothesline with wooden clothespins.

Years later, I wondered what had happened to that black iron wash pot? Today, people would consider it an antique. Later, Donald L and Alvin, told me that the pot cracked and fell apart because of the many washings and the fires that were built around it. My brothers used the stove to heat the dishwater, then poured the hot water into the dishpan to wash the dishes. A huge butane gas tank was located directly behind our home. A big white man delivered our gas monthly, on Saturdays. All my siblings would stand around, waiting to hear my mother's voice. She always had to argue with him because she said he was not filling the gas tank to capacity; however, he charged us for a full tank. I did not know why Mama felt this man always tried to cheat her out of a full tank of gas. Later, I realized Mama knew how long a tank of gas should last to supply our home since we used it for our kitchen stove.

They placed the Dearborn heater in Mama and Deddy's front bedroom, and a small heater in the children's middle bedroom. There were three large rooms in our new house. At the front of the house, which faced Humbert Street, we had two entrance doors; one led into the living room, and one led into my parents' bedroom. In the living room, we had a couch that unfolded into a bed, a piano, and a breakfast table that ET made in his shop class at school. We were a resourceful family who learned to share. The sound of my mother playing the piano still resonates in my ears. We used the space in the middle of the house as a large bedroom, which also served as our kitchen. This room housed three enormous beds. All the children were in the middle bedroom. Bed space was tight, Alvin and I shared a bed. Donald L and Bruce shared a bed and Adolphus, Howard and E.T. shared a big iron bed.

Growing fresh vegetables was important in my family, and we all played a part in planting and cultivating our garden. My mom assigned each of us a specific vegetable to grow, and we learned how to dig the soil and plant the seeds. I particularly enjoyed growing tomatoes, onions, cucumbers, green beans, sweet potatoes, turnip and collard greens, purple hull peas, herbs, and squash. Our garden had every vegetable one could think of. Whenever I needed a quick snack, I would grab a cucumber and sprinkle some salt on it to taste. Across the back of our property, fruit trees produced peaches, plums, and pears, while in the front yard grew a tall pecan tree. Fig trees grew on the east side of the house. We made sure not to waste any of the edible items. Mama canned peaches, plums, pears, and fig preserves. I can taste those fig preserves and smell the homemade buttered biscuits as I share those moments.

We had cured meat from the country and real-live chickens–pork from the hogs, steak, bacon, and more. I became frightened when we had chicken for our meal. Mama would catch a chicken running around the backyard, grab it by the neck, and wring its neck around and around until the chicken was dead. She immediately placed it in hot water as we gazed in amazement at the feathers as they fell off the chicken's body. You talk about good fried chicken. It would be finger-licking good. On weekends, for breakfast, we enjoyed homemade biscuits, bacon, eggs, and meat. Sometimes, we had steak on weekends. These were memorable times because Mama did not have time to cook breakfast throughout the week. Do not get me wrong; sometimes we only had bread, syrup, and pinto beans with cornbread.

Old Lee, our dog, protected our family and home for years before a tragedy occurred. I was young, but I remember what happened. It was a sad day. Dad accidentally killed our dog when he backed the car up. My brothers and I built a casket for Old Lee. My mother told us to throw the dog away because dogs do not have a soul, but we buried him under the hill across the street where we lived. Our dog's burial was one of the saddest moments of our lives.

Mama signed up for the Christmas Goodfellows in October or November to get toys, food, and vouchers to purchase clothes for all her children during the holidays. Back in the day, the Goodfellows worker visited homes to see if the families qualified for the vouchers.

Mama always knew the date and time the lady would visit. She kept us home that day. The lady always asked, "Do you need food and clothes?"

I always replied, "Our family needs food, clothes and money for new shoes." My mother and I had rehearsed my reply prior to the visit. There was no doubt about the need for financial help. Like clockwork, every Christmas Eve, the big truck would swing around the corner at Humbert and Merrick. The delivery men would jump out of the truck, grab crates of fruit and boxes of food, and place them on the porch. The vouchers were in an envelope with our parents' names on them.

Mama took us downtown to Everybody's Department Store to exchange the vouchers for shoes and clothes. It was a joyous occasion. Christmas was an exciting time for the Chadwick family. We had a tradition of walking under the hill every Christmas and cutting down our Christmas tree. All the siblings took part. We dragged the tree up the hill into the living room and placed it on our glass-top table. We painted the leafless tree white, and attached beautiful red and blue bulbs on each limb. Our family stood around the tree and sang "Jingle Bells" on Christmas morning. How I wish I had a photo of our homemade Christmas tree. No one ever knew my siblings and I cut down the trees from under the hill.

Ever since I was in first grade, I wanted a doll. My parents could not afford one. When I was 10, my dream came true. On Christmas morning, what do you think was under the tree with my name on the box? It was the long-awaited doll. I never played dollhouse, though. I did not tell my parents, at ten-years-old, I thought I was too old for a doll. However, I placed the 24-inch-tall figure in the corner and observed the beauty. When I left home, I left it behind. Years later, I saw it and the once beautiful doll, now had a bald head.

Donald L, Alvin, Bruce, and I eagerly anticipated our weekly allowance. Deddy would give us two nickels on Fridays. Donald L shared his nickel with Bruce, and I shared mine with Alvin. That was a treat, and we always waited for it. Duke's Grocery store was located across the street and down the left side of the road by a big tree. We bought giant Jack Cookies for a nickel. Each bag contained five cookies, which means we got two and a half cookies each. We ate them all day and had to hide whatever we bought, or someone would eat them as the others slept.

Each summer, Mama sent Donald L, Alvin, Bruce, and me to spend a couple of weeks with her father, Papa Harry Woods, in Longview, Texas. Papa Harry practiced medicine with herbs. He always wore a suit. He grew herbs in his house, and little jars of greenery grew all over his place, including on the windowsills.

One day, I asked Papa Harry, "What do you do with the weeds you bring home?"

Papa Harry answered, "Child, these are not weeds. This is my medicine!"

He went out into the woods, picked herbs from nature, and brought crates of herbs home to heal his clients. The people called him "The Medicine Man."

The four of us had to sweep the yard daily until it had no loose sand—just hard dirt. That was something we preferred not to do.

Usually, during the summer, my older sister from Dallas brought her kids to visit. They called my mother, "Mama Lula." Well, one could tell when the grandkids were in the house. Those were the times when we had to fight for our existence.

My oldest niece, Ella, was two years younger than me. She was a pretty girl with long red hair like her mother and was loud and boisterous. Ella was a fighter and was not afraid of no one or anything. She would fearlessly fight anyone for what she believed in or wanted, which made her the complete opposite of her reserved and quiet mother. Whenever my sister, Aldotsie, visited my mother, Ella would fight with us. Although I was not a fighter, I did not let her beat my ass. Bruce was always there to fight her, but he couldn't even take her down. I had to help him keep Ella from beating him up. During one of our fights, I told her to pick on someone her size. One time, Ella hit Bruce in the head with a toaster, and Donald L had to rescue him.

One sibling left the nest. Mossey graduated from I.M. Terrell in 1952. I believed my sister was the most attractive girl at I.M. Terrell. She had a curvy figure and her skin was high yellow like my mother's. Her long, straight black hair fell effortlessly to her hips, and she had a long line of admirers. We could not speak incorrect English around Mossey. She would immediately correct the sentence; then we had to repeat the correct words. She was a stickler for speaking standard English. Mossey communicated with a big, wide smile, and that made it difficult to get upset with her. The owner of the Lake Como Newsstand, where she worked, presented her to society as a debutante through the Fort Worth Assembly. The Fort Worth Assembly is one of the city's most prestigious social/cultural organizations. Founded in 1941, the Assembly advances and recognizes African American girls and young women. Her dress was a floor-length, pure white ball gown made with white net material, accentuated by long white gloves with white pearls.

Who is a debutante? Webster's Dictionary defines a debutante as a young woman formally entering society. A Fort Worth Assembly Debutante is a young woman of excellent moral character aged 17- 23 and currently enrolled at an accredited college or university. Mossey graduated with a four-year scholarship to Texas Southern University in Houston, where Aunt Christine lived. Her goal was to become a medical doctor. She continued her education, completed her internship an St. Paul Minnesota Hospital, and became a medical doctor. Dr. Mossey Chadwick Haynes practiced medicine at St. Paul and married Dr. Leroy Haynes in August 1963.

One of my fondest moments was when Mossey returned home one Fourth of July. I was ten years old, too old to be disciplined by my sister, or so I thought. After all, Mossey no longer lived at home. One evening, she asked me to do the dishes, but I kept swinging around the pecan tree in our front yard. She asked me two or three more times, and I boldly screamed, "Heifer, leave me alone!" I had heard girls at school use this word. That story did not end well. She struck me, knocked me on my butt, and told me to move. I gladly hopped up, ran to the kitchen, and completed the task. My bottom was sore for several days! The second lesson learned was never to use a word you heard others use without knowing the definition. Sadly, Mossey died during childbirth on September 13, 1964, and at her funeral, her baby girl was placed in the foot of her casket.

Alvin was excited when Mama enrolled him in Como Elementary in 1952. That year, however, Mama became ill with heart problems. Dad took her to Dr. Ransom's Hospital for Blacks in downtown Fort Worth. The doctor gave up on Mama and told her she would die. All I could hear was my mother praying, "The devil is a liar." She told the doctor that her Lord and Savior, Jesus Christ, had the last words. We all grew up believing in the power of prayer and God miraculously healed my mother. She got up from her sick bed and continued working.

After Mossey left, E.T. was the oldest sibling at home and he dominated most people with his loud voice. He was a handsome athlete, a good golfer, and a talented basketball player. E.T. was the tallest in the family at 6'5" and the second in the family to attain a college degree. He had to babysit the younger children when Mother and Deddy went to work. Our cousin, Billy Gray, helped E.T. get a job caddying at Colonial Country Club when he was in the ninth grade. With this money, E.T. had funds for school necessities and clothes. My other brothers were too young to start caddying.

When Howard was about thirteen years old, E.T. took him to the golf course and trained him to be a caddy. Deddy only allowed Howard to go to the golf course three times a week. Howard left Colonial Country Club and started caddying at Ridglea Country Club, and he took Adolphus with him. Adolphus did not like caddying and Bruce was too young to hang with the older brothers.

In 1954, my parents purchased the lot next door, west of our property, at 5104 Humbert. Now, our family owned the land from 5100 Humbert to 5104 Humbert. On this property was a red house that looked like a train caboose where Mrs. Bass lived with her four girls, Erie, Gladys, Shirlene, and Maggie. I had a fun time playing with the girls, and hide and seek became a daily routine with my friend, Lenet, who lived across the street. Mrs. Bass's son, Clarence, rented the caboose from my parents. This family was terrific renters, with a pleasant attitude all the time. When the Bass family eventually moved out, my mother remodeled the caboose and turned it into a church. That was all we needed: a church right next door. Mama was a missionary who had another missionary friend we called Sister Mattie. She joined Mama in creating the church. Mama and Sister Mattie made me and my three younger brothers, get on our knees and tarry (wait on God) until we spoke in other tongues. You had to tarry to be filled with the Holy Ghost. Then you got up and ate grapes.

My brothers were wise; they would tarry for about 30 minutes, then fall out and start speaking in other tongues. While they ate grapes, I was still on my knees. I did not get up until church was over. By then, I was exhausted. Of course my brothers were only pretending. Still, I never received anything by staying on my knees "tarrying," except Sister Mattie's spit all in my face.

I can hear her now, "Thank you, Jesus! Thank you, Jesus! Thank Him! Thank Him!"

Bruce could pretend and make you think his actions came directly from the Holy Spirit. Once I heard him fall out, and he rolled all over the floor. Bruce repeatedly rolled his tongue. He sounded like he was speaking in a foreign language. I gave Bruce the name, "The Great Pretender."

When Mama purchased the lot, she bought a septic tank and inserted it underground on our home's west side. Then, Deddy had an inside bathroom added to our house with a water heater and a door. Oh Lord, what a wonderful blessing! An inside toilet meant no more turning your butt up to the air in the outhouse. It also meant a bathtub. We didn't have to heat our water and bathe in a tin tub. We all took turns washing dishes after meals. The sibling who cleaned the kitchen heated water and poured the water into the dishpan on the stove. Deddy added an ivory-colored sink set on wooden legs, and we heated the water and poured it into the sink to wash dishes. The water ran outside into a hole located under the kitchen window in the backyard.

Knox Tucker and Jap Jones were E.T.'s basketball coaches at I.M. Terrell High School. He started playing basketball at three years old and continued throughout high school. He won the majority of his competitive games. He graduated from high school in 1955. Deddy took him to Texas Christian University (TCU) and asked about E.T. enrolling because of his academics and basketball skills. TCU turned Deddy away. However, Texas College offered E.T. a full four-year basketball scholarship, and he accepted it and played basketball for that school.

He then became a coach and taught several sports, including golf. He taught school after college and later entered the armed forces. After his honorable discharge, he moved to California. There, he played basketball for the L.A. Stars and later for the San Antonio Spurs (ADA League). E.T. retired from basketball and started his own business, in California, Chadwick's Furniture. He operated his business until he returned to Fort Worth in 1983 with his wife, Bertha, and five children: Neloice Faith, Edward Thomas Jr., Courtney, Nilliah Jovan, and Jehrime. They moved to Everman, Texas, where he currently lives.

Growing up in the 50s, my brothers walked to Ridglea Country Club. They had to walk the length of the seven-foot Ridglea Wall to get to work. Someone created a shortcut by cutting a hole in the fence so people could get to the golf course in less time. Earlier, the long walk often caused the boys to be late getting to the club. Streetlights came to the area in the 60s, along with paved streets.

In 1971, the brick wall came down after the Como neighborhood protested about it to the City Council in 1969. It was a means of segregation and discrimination. The sewer line was built in the 70s.

In 1954, Deddy had another big room added to the east side of our home. It was a kitchen, with a partition in the middle to make another bedroom. I don't remember why, but Deddy never finished the kitchen sink cabinet. It sat on four legs, with a door in the front and the sink on top. In that kitchen, Mama taught me to cook and I stirred her cake batter. Eventually, I cooked for the family while my mother and father worked.

My brothers who were not employed, cleaned the house. Since it took longer to finish my job, I cooked early to complete the meals before Mama returned home. My brothers' task was easy because they had a system. Usually, they watched for my mother to top the hill behind our house and then hurriedly cleaned the house. They played and fought each other most of the day. About 30 minutes before Mother arrived home from work, the boys called for a truce to gain time to clean up. They kept their eyes on the hill behind our house, a trail shortcut that ended in our backyard.

Still, Bruce always got in trouble. I told my mother everything I heard and about every fight I witnessed during the day. I made sure to catch her as she walked down the hill. No one could beat me getting to her first and I filled her in on whatever happened between us during the day. I took it upon myself to make a daily report. When I added extra "yeast," my mother paid much more attention. The more colorful adjectives helped my reports. My brothers accused me of being a tattletale. Of course, neither of them could hit me because I was a girl. All I had to do was tell my mother that one of my brothers had hit me in the stomach. That meant someone was going to get a whipping. Growing up with six brothers was challenging; I had no sister to share my female issues with.

CHAPTER FOUR

When Roots Become Wings

My Mama never missed a day from work that I can remember. She went to work in the rain, shine, sleet, or snow. When it snowed, she would wrap her feet in cloth so that she wouldn't slip and fall, and that kept her feet warm.

Howard graduated from Como High School in 1957 and left home when I was fourteen. Howard was a charming, good-looking man who had a way with women. He was a professional golfer and played in two United States Openings. He was the most talented golfer among the Chadwick boys. Besides having an easy-going personality, curly hair, and light brown skin, he was a hard worker. Despite being the shortest family member, he was always determined to succeed.

He married Lillie Geiger right out of high school. They had four children: Deborah, Linda, Stacy, and Shawn. Howard had two additional children, Kathy Houston Hughes and D'Vonte Chadwick. Golf was in his blood, and he became a professional golfer. He played golf at the Z Boaz Golf Club, and they hired him as the Head Pro. All of my brothers, except Frank and Alvin, learned to play golf and caddied at the Ridglea Country Club.

Alvin and Donald L were about eleven or twelve years old when they started chopping cotton in the summer months in order to make summer money for school. I, on the other hand, loved to read books and look at pictures when I was home.

Whenever there were school events, my mother allowed me to go, and Adolphus always accompanied me. I appreciated his company because he was an attractive, tall, and cheerful person with silky salt-and-pepper hair who never got angry. He had a deep voice, a weird laugh when he told jokes and, like our father, talkative. The girls flocked to him whenever we went out, but I never told my mother. His male friends were the most popular boys in Como.

Adolphus Chadwick and I dancing at a Como Christmas party.

On Sundays, Adolphus and I would sneak to the Shelter House in Como Park, where the students gathered to dance and have fun. During that time, most students in Como learned how to do the latest dances, and the Swing Out was the most popular. The DJ's loud, hot music echoed throughout the park. Whenever someone extended their hand to dance, I said, "Yes, yes." I never turned down a dance opportunity. My parents did not know we snuck into the park every Sunday afternoon, and I dared not tell them. I appreciate him for allowing me to tag along. I became an excellent dancer. Today, I still dance.

Adolphus graduated from Como High School in 1959. During his time in school, he actively took part in basketball and golf and was always willing to help those in need. Later, he left home to attend Texas College in Tyler, Texas. However, after two years, he realized there were better paths for him than college. He entered barber school, where he met and married Dorothy Quartz. They briefly lived with Mama until the Army drafted him, and then Dorothy returned home to stay with her mother. They had two boys, Douglas and Reginald. After his return from the Army, he and Dorothy divorced. This time allowed him to purchase his own barbershop, and he became a successful businessman. He married Gwendolyn Washington and had two sons, Keith Eugene and Kevin Adolphus Chadwick.

Unfortunately, Gwendolyn died. In 1982, Adolphus reunited with and married his childhood sweetheart, Winstona Laythette. She brought two daughters, Kimona Kim Dixon and Melody Michon Scurlock, to the union. Our household dwindled. Four siblings were now at home: Bruce, Alvin, Donald L, and me.

During the 1959 sports season, I was a football cheerleader. My mother was unaware I was a cheerleader and she would not have allowed it had she known. Dancing allowed me to make the cheerleading team, along with the long black hair down my back. Then, everyone called me "high yellow." I was a favorite with my teachers; I could grade papers, but I could not miss a class. On football game evenings, I packed my cheerleader outfit and left it at my cousin's home. After school, I got dressed at Gray's house and snuck off to the football games. I knew every cheer and I danced all over the field, shouting "Go Lions, Go!"

Then, It was time to go home. When I arrived home at night, my mother awaited me with her belt. That was not bad; I would stop hurting after five to ten minutes. I never missed a game, although

I would get the belt each time I came home late. Some friends labeled me a "slow learner in football and cheerleading." Donald L and Alvin were my biggest supporters.

My father never whipped me. He threatened me by saying, "Girl, if you don't straighten up, I am gonna make you break outta that back door!"

Mama was an independent woman. In 1960, she purchased a 1953 Chevrolet. Now, she could drive to work and attend school activities when she was off.

Bruce graduated from Como High School in May 1963. The Chadwick brothers are all good-looking, and Bruce is no exception. He was well-built, light complected, and had black curly hair like our mother's. Bruce was athletic, played basketball and golf, and had good business skills. People knew him for his generosity and he would give you the shirt off his back. He had a loud, sexy voice like Deddy, and he loved to talk, tell jokes and laugh. Girls were interested in him, but he only had eyes for one. He eventually married Joyce Malone, his childhood sweetheart, and brought Joyce to live with Mama and the boys for about six months. Shortly after his marriage, Bruce left home and went to California to go to school and get a good-paying job. After a short time, he returned to Texas and moved to a house in Fort Worth. He and Joyce had two children, Bruce Harold Jr. and Tonja. Bruce enrolled in a furniture upholstery school. His career path was clear; he loved working with furniture. After briefly working with an upholstery company, he became an entrepreneur and opened his own successful upholstery shop, Chadwick's Furniture.

Alvin and Donald L were now the only siblings left at home. They were the baby boys and their relationship was not good at all. Alvin was possessive of all his belongings, but Donald L always wore Alvin's clothes to school. One day, Donald L wore Alvin's socks. Alvin went to Donald L's classroom, called him out, and told him to get his "ass" out of his socks. As they grew older, their relationship worsened. One day, they were in the kitchen, and

Alvin threw a butcher knife at Donald L, and barely missed his head. That was the last straw for Mama.

Alvin was talented in music, and he never took part in athletics. He played for churches in East Fort Worth. In the ninth grade, Alvin started playing for Rev. James Kennard's Bibleway Baptist Church, across the street from the Cavile Housing projects in the Stop-six neighborhood. The pastor paid Alvin $7.50 a week and provided transportation to and from his home in Lake Como. With the money he earned, Alvin purchased clothing for school and other activities. Alvin played for the church until he left Texas for Los Angeles, California.

He also delivered newspapers during high school to earn extra money. He had a charming appearance, always carried a big smile, had light brown skin, straight hair, and wore colorful and pretty clothes. Alvin had a more feminine personality than my other brothers, but he never played with dolls or other girly toys in childhood. Despite his feminine tendencies, I loved Alvin unconditionally. After he graduated from high school in May 1965, our mother arranged for him to go to California to live with our brother E.T. and attend college.

Alvin entered the Barber College of Los Angeles and received his master barber and beautician licenses. Shortly after arriving in California, he took a job playing the piano for Magnolia Baptist Church and played there for 20 years until he moved back to Fort Worth, Texas. While he was in California, he opened a shop in Los Angeles called "Alvin's Hair Clinic of Los Angeles." When the family traveled to California to visit him, we loved the opportunity to get our hair styled by Alvin in his famous shop. He was successful.

Alvin and his friend, Jeff, came home every year to visit. He always stayed at my house on Ramey Avenue because others did not welcome gays. As I stated earlier, it did not bother me that he was gay; he was my brother. After Jeff died, Alvin met Captain. Later, in 1992, they sold their California homes and businesses and returned home to help me care for Mama. Once he returned to Texas, Morningside Methodist Church on Evans Avenue hired Alvin as their pianist.

Donald L, the youngest, became the only sibling at home with Mama and Deddy. While Deddy was asleep, Donald L would take his car and practice driving. He took time to play with my son, Edmond, and his big red ball. Edmond loved his ball. One day, Donald L was watching him but lost track of him. The family became worried; they all looked for him but could not find him. They kept calling his name, but he was nowhere in sight. Finally, Donald L opened the doors that housed the kitchen sink. He found Edmond standing under the kitchen sink in his diaper and house shoes with a big grin from cheek to cheek.

Donald L traveled everywhere with Deddy, and listened to all the stories about our family history. They became two peas in a pod. The conversations became all about family memories and the future. Donald L was blessed with opportunities we didn't have, and had a unique bond with my father. Now, my father could treat his baby boy as an only child.

Edmond in his diaper and house shoes.

He married Helen Malone in 1967 and moved to a home in Lake Como. That same year, Deddy died. One child, Sharlene, was born to Donald L and Helen. In 1986, Donald L rented out his home in Lake Como and purchased a home in the Meadowbrook neighborhood in east Fort Worth. He worked as a custodian in the Birdville School District, where one teacher encouraged him to attend college. He enrolled in North Texas

University while he worked in the school district and he graduated with a degree in Political Science and Sociology.

He owned several businesses: Top Notch Janitorial, Top Notch Investments, Chadwick Earth Removal, Transit Systems, Mary Kay Consultant, and Day Trading Stock, Fort Worth, Texas.

Lockheed Martin offered Donald L a job. After working 40 years for Lockheed as an employee and supervisor, he retired. At Lockheed, he learned to invest and be a businessman. If we needed to know information about finance and real estate, we could call him. He was the overseer of our family property. My parents taught their children how to work hard and accumulate assets; ten of my brothers and sisters became entrepreneurs. More importantly, our parents set examples and taught us morals, values, character, honesty, integrity, respect, and love for family, one another, and others. Mama's statement to my siblings resonates today in my ear, "Learning how to read is power!"

My oldest sister, Aldotsie Chadwick Davis (Carlee Davis), lived in Dallas, Texas. She had five children: Ella Weese Davis, Harold Lynn Davis, Dorothy Davis Titus, Carlee Davis Jr., and Steve Radford Davis. She was the sole possessor of a soft voice and long red hair that cascaded down her back and caused her to stand out in our family. She had our family's physical features, including a captivating smile, shapely legs, and a delightful yellow complexion that added to her charm. Her love for children and her innate kindness and generosity were evident in her actions. Her slow, unhurried demeanor and her southern drawl often led her to be fashionably late for church, work, and events. Aldotsie was the proud owner of the Colonial Barber and Beauty Salon in Dallas, Texas.

One day, the family recently received news from my older brother, Frank, who had relocated to Houston, Texas, from Diana, and had found a job at the Frito factory. Frank, the oldest son, often considered the head of the Dock Tucker Chadwick family, was proud to be a sharply dressed individual who always wore a suit.

He had an emotional connection with all his family members. Frank known to be quite handsome, had a heavy voice, was easygoing, and had high yellow skin and black curly hair like our mother. He had a musical gift and enjoyed singing and traveling with a quartet. Frank mailed Fritos home every month. We always watched the mail for those delicious Fritos. Two children were born to him, Thomas Gene and Cynthia.

My next oldest sister, Mary Virginia Chadwick Edwards (J.C. Edwards), lived in Dallas, Texas. Two children were born to her: Carolyn Edwards Bullock and Douglas Charles Edwards Sr. Virginia loved to talk as much and loudly as my brothers. With her southern drawl, it wasn't easy to keep up with them. She sported a head full of long black silky hair, brown skin, a beautiful smile, big legs, and a shape that rocked the boys far and near. Her spirit of love for others and building relationships was vital for Virginia. She owned the Ewing Avenue Beauty Salon in Dallas, Texas.

CHAPTER FIVE

Dock Tucker and Lula Mae Woods Chadwick

My Father

Dock Tucker Chadwick, was born in Panola County, Texas, on July 29, 1906. He was the eighth child in a family of thirteen, born to Dock Chadwick (April 11, 1867 - November 9, 1918) and Laura Jane Matkins. After Laura Jane's death, Dock married Lela Smith and had three more children: Howard, Dock, and Weldon. Dock and his brother, John, were the only two people of my family in Texas after the 1889 land run in Oklahoma.

They donated land for the first school to the black community, known as Holland Quarters (formerly the Holland Plantation). This land provided a school and a home for the teachers who taught the Holland Quarters' children. The brothers also donated land for Holland Quarters Cemetery. Dock and John were hard workers with business insight, and they accumulated land that they shared with the community. The family buried Dock in the family plot in Holland Quarters Cemetery after he died in 1918. As was the family tradition, he left each of his 13 children 50 acres of land.

Dock Tucker Chadwick, the man we called "Deddy" was the epitome of a commanding presence, with a stature that spoke of strength and reliability. His broad shoulders could seemingly bear the weight of the world, yet they were always ready to offer a comforting embrace to his children. His thick eyebrows were like the expressive brushstrokes of an artist, framing his kind, deep-set eyes that sparkled with warmth and wisdom.

Deddy's skin was a rich, brown hue, a testament to a life lived fully under the sun's embrace, and his tall frame moved with a grace that belied his size. His hair, as black as the midnight sky, always remained neatly groomed, with a bald spot on top that complemented his handsome features. Despite his robust appearance, he was the gentlest of giants. His voice, a soothing baritone, had the power to calm the stormiest of days.

He was a man who fiercely loved his children, with a tenderness that was as natural to him as breathing. His love was a constant, unwavering force that guided and protected them. Deddy had a natural sense of style, always dressed impeccably for every occasion, whether it was a dressy event or a casual family gathering. His attire was not only about looking good, but about showing respect for the people and the moments that made up his life.

Dock Tucker Chadwick was not just a father; he was a beacon of love and stability, a man whose presence was a source of comfort and joy to those of us who were lucky enough to call him our dad.

My parents married on March 1, 1925. They were the proud parents of twelve children, and both of my parents came from prominent families. My mother had nine siblings, and my dad grew up with thirteen siblings, six half-brothers, and sisters. Deddy grew up surrounded by acres of land, cattle, hogs, chickens, and gardens owned by his parents. He left Carthage, Texas, in 1939 or 1940 and people knew him for his baseball skills. While in Carthage, sometimes he traveled with a baseball league and sent money home to Mama.

My father and mother, Dock Tucker and Lula Mae Woods Chadwick.

Sisters: Aldotsie Chadwick Davis, me, and Virginia Chadwick Edwards.

My sister, Dr. Mossey Chadwick Haynes.

My sister, Mary Virginia Edwards loved styling hair. She used me as her model in hair shows in Dallas. I love this old fashion hairstyle.

My brothers standing (left to right): Edward Thomas Chadwick Sr.(E.T.), Frank Thomas Chadwick, Howard Rosco Chadwick and Donald L Chadwick. Front row (left to right) Bruce Harold Chadwick, Adolphus Chadwick, and Alvin Chadwick.

I never heard my mother and father argue. However, she once agitatedly called Deddy's name. I know she was mad because she rolled the "r" in his name, "Tuckerrrr!" Unfortunately, I could not make out what they were saying because they both mumbled. After a while, everything became quiet, and you could hear a pin drop. When they both emerged from their conversation, they had a smile on their faces, and I always wondered what happened.

My dad was a hard worker who landed a job at Traders Oil in Fort Worth. After working there for two years, he broke his leg, could not walk, and did not return to the job. After a long recovery, he worked at Ridglea Country Club as a waiter. Later, he landed another job working at night at the fertilizer plant on the north side, and worked there for about five years. During a rainstorm, while loading the fertilizer hopper, lightning struck him. Because of that accident, Deddy lost his ability to work and his employment was terminated. He received compensation for his injuries, though. Deddy always complained about his stomach problems, and we always thought that the lightning had burned his stomach when it struck him. He was a dependable and committed worker and never missed a day when he was working. He believed in the Bible and supported Mama dearly; however, he only attended church on special occasions or for a funeral.

My father bragged a lot and had a gift for storytelling. He boasted about his children's success and how he had lived and played ball in East Texas. I know God blessed my father with the gift of gab. My brothers inherited the same gift of gab. I can hear him now with his loud and heavy voice. His friends listened to him throughout the Domino Shack. Every Saturday night, he played dominos at the Domino Shack on Bonnell. He could play dominoes and talk for hours while his friends laughed at his jokes. Almost no one could beat him playing dominoes and he taught all his boys how to play except Frank and Alvin. I am curious to know how they missed out. Deddy was a free and happy man who also enjoyed his alcoholic spirits. At all our family gatherings, I listened to my brothers, especially Frank, Adolphus, and Bruce, as they told jokes about our family. We laughed until we cried. The joy from our family gatherings and memories are priceless. I always loved to be with my family.

My parents believed in education. Education for the Chadwick family was a priority. If my parents had to attend school for any wrongdoings, they would embarrass us and whip us in the classroom. Mama was a strict disciplinarian. Once we got home, she would whip our butts again. This only happened once to Bruce, but never again. He was a fast learner.

On Friday nights, Deddy loved to watch television. Around 1956, Mossey surprised us with a black-and-white television. He loved boxing and when he watched it on television, he stood in front of the set and threw punches at the boxers. We watched and said, "Hit him, Deddy. Hit him!" We giggled as he danced around the television. His routine usually comprised coming home from the Domino Shack on Saturday nights, sitting in the house, and watching television.

For me, I could not wait to hear the theme song, "William Tell Overture." I knew the Lone Ranger and Tonto were on the screen.

Many evenings, when it was cold, he came home and sat before the heater in the middle bedroom as though he was in pain. Deddy sat with his shirt off. My brothers and I could see the perspiration on Deddy's face and back. "Deddy, what is wrong? Are you hurting?" I asked, but he wouldn't say one word. My brothers and I sat at his feet. Deddy loved his children and Lula Mae, our mother.

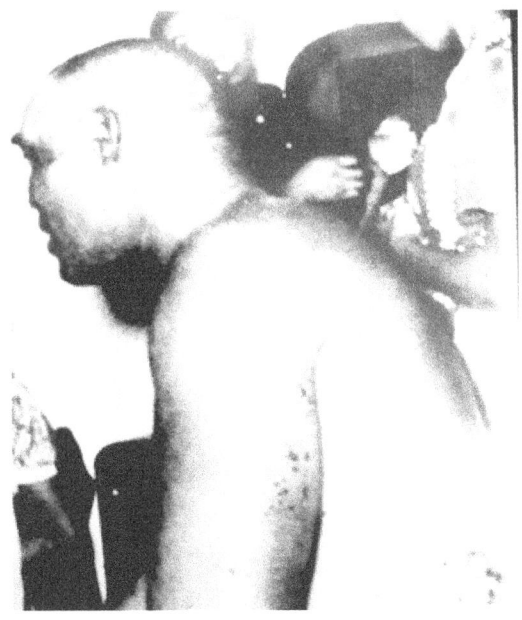

Me, standing over my daddy with his shirt off while he watched television. Deddy was a big, strong man.

He always tried to teach us games or a skill. My parents encouraged all of us to be the best we could be. Not only were they business savvy, they had common sense. They instilled in us the importance of family, education, and always working hard to accomplish your goals.

My parents and Donald L were always ready to babysit and keep my children while I was in nursing school. When my parents retired, they had accumulated property in Lake Como and property in Diana, Texas, not including the homestead. They accomplished this, although Deddy only completed the fifth grade and Mama only completed the eight grade. (She later returned to school and received her G.E.D.)

My Mother

My mother, Lula Mae Woods Chadwick, was born July 5, 1907, in Panola County, Texas, to Harry and Mossey Woods. She attended the Holland Quarters School in Panola County. Early in her life, she became a member of Pine Grove Baptist Church in Carthage, Texas. She joined the Shady Grove Baptist Church when she moved to Diana, Texas. My mother loved talking to others about the Bible, and she talked to whomever listened. In her search for spiritual fulfillment, she joined the Macedonia Apostolic Church, where she experienced baptism in Jesus' name and being filled with the Holy Ghost.

Before Mama became dedicated to the church, her hair was in a bob cut, and she wore thigh-high net hose with a garter belt, and high heels. Lula Mae Woods Chadwick was a woman whose beauty was as radiant as her spirit. Her long, black, curly, wavy hair cascaded around her shoulders like a soft, inviting halo. Her complexion, a delicate shade often described as high yellow, glowed with an inner light that was only enhanced by the bold red lipstick she favored. It was a color that spoke of her confidence and vitality. My mother was 5 '6," with big legs and hips, and built like an hourglass. My mother though, had a generous nature and always cared for others. She extended her kindness to all children, not only her own. Her compassion knew no bounds. My mother applied water and oil to her hair, brushed it, and the curls fell in place. She had her mother's features and could have easily passed for a white woman in the right setting. She often found a job with little effort. Her attitude and personality were always positive, and she smiled beautifully.

Yet, despite her warmth and tenderness, Mama also had a reputation for firmness. She had a strength that was the foundation of her household, and she guided her family with a strict, yet loving hand. Her discipline was a testament to her deep care and desire to see her children grow into their best selves.

Macedonia Apostle Church, in Diana, Texas, is where she gave her life to Christ as a faithful member. My dad was a dedicated supporter of my mother and a family man. He cared for his family the best he could with the education he had.

As a Christian, she believed in going to church. Mama attended Crouch Memorial Church of God in Christ on Goodman Street. Elder Crouch served as pastor after we arrived in Fort Worth. Other times, she attended Twelfth Street Pentecostal Church on 12th Street near downtown, where Elder North served as pastor. We attended church every day of the week except on Saturday. All my siblings, if not working on Sunday, attended church with my mother. We sat in the back and worked on our school assignments. My mother did not play; there were no options for handling our assigned duties and school assignments.

In 1965, Deddy had a stroke. Mama kept him at home, in a hospital bed set up in the living room. All the children came home to see him; however, all his care fell on Donald L and Mama. Two years later, he died on July 13, 1967, at the age of 60. Donald L, the baby boy, had just married and moved to a home in Lake Como. The morning Deddy died, Mama called Donald L to come and help her with him. When he arrived, Deddy asked him to take him around to the west side of the house and put him in his chair.

Donald L stated, "When we were halfway around the house, Deddy closed his eyes in death." That was an emotional moment for him.

My parents shared their lives for forty-four years. I watched my parents over the years, and one of their greatest strengths was their ability to build strong relationships. Their actions, such as sharing our food and clothing with those in need, left a lasting impression on me. It did not matter who the person was or where they came from; if anyone needed any help, my parents were always willing to help. Their selflessness and compassion shaped my values and continue to guide my actions today.

That quality rubbed off on me, and I help others in need without hesitation. One must be careful, of course, about how you help people on the street. If they have the sign on the corner that says, "Will work for food," pick up a McDonald's hamburger and drop it off to them. Building relationships is a valuable asset, and I take pride in connecting with people. When I see people at the gas station wanting money for gas; I always use my card and give them gas, never cash.

One time, my friend needed a coat, and I had two or three coats. She came to my house and I gave her one. That character trait came from my mother. Also I learned from her the importance

Papa Harry and Mrs. Gentry Wood's home. (Personal collection of Donald L Chadwick)

My grandmother, Mossey Woods.

My grandparents: my mama's father, Papa Harry Woods and her stepmother, Mrs. Gentry Woods.

of conversation. Talking with others brings me joy and a feeling of self-worth. More than that, it helps combat loneliness and improves mental health.

As members of the holiness church, we took part in service each Sunday for four to five hours. At our church, the parents sat in the front row, and the children sat in the row directly behind them. When we lived in Diana, Texas, my mother provided Bruce, Alvin, Donald L, and me with snacks and two hamburgers during the service on one particular day. We divided the two hamburgers between us four children. Mama gave each child half of a hamburger. Angrily, I threw my half on the floor and told her, "I do not want that; I want a whole hamburger."

I never saw the hand that struck me from the front seat, but I felt it. Mama never turned around; she threw her hand behind her back, knocked me onto the floor, and told me to "pick up the food and eat it." That taught me to be grateful for whatever one shares with me or gives me. I learned to say, "Thank you." My brothers sat on the seat and giggled as I picked myself up off the floor. Mama also loved playing the piano; she taught herself how to play. Members of the church would sing, and she would hit the notes, regardless of how the melody sounded. She wanted to give all her children opportunities to participate in the arts. Mama registered Bruce, Alvin, and Donald L, and me in music lessons with Mrs. Barker, who lived in the neighborhood. Mrs. Barker was a mean lady, but an excellent music teacher. She would hit the knuckles on our fingers with a ruler when we played the wrong key. I took part in my first music recital at the age of 13 in 1956. We eventually stopped taking music lessons because of a lack of interest or knuckles.

However, Mama transferred Alvin to a new music teacher. Mrs. Langston lived on the east side. He started playing for the church in Stop-Six in the 11th grade. Alvin played in the school band through

My first music recital at the age of 13. My mother took Mossey's net presentation gown and remade it for my recital dress. This is the photo used for the cover of my book.

high school. Earlier, on our arrival in Fort Worth, Mama started interviewing for a job. There were several jobs available, including cleaning homes and cleaning for a restaurant. Mama washed pots and pans for the Old Plantation Restaurant. She got E.T. a job across the street at the Pig Stand as a soda fountain worker. Later, Mama did "day work" for affluent white couples. She sometimes cooked for the families at her job. She loved cooking desserts.

The sweet aroma of fresh coconut often wafted through the house as my mother taught me how to make desserts. Whenever she called me to the kitchen, she'd say, "Chris, let's whip up a cake." My mouth watered as I gathered all the ingredients. If we were missing something, my mother would find a substitute. Together, we made delicious four-layer cakes, pound cakes, coconut cakes, pineapple upside-down cakes, and chocolate cakes. Looking back, I could have used an electric mixer; my arm felt as if it would fall off while mixing the thick cake batter. As she taught me to cook, I learned the true meaning of a "pinch." My mother always kept plenty of flour and food ingredients in our kitchen. I have continued that tradition in my own home. However, whenever my mother asked me to add a pinch of salt, baking powder, or soda to the flour, I would ask, "Mama, how much is a pinch?"

She would pinch her fingers together, show me some salt and say, "Chris, this is a pinch." Even today, I struggle to cook using just a pinch of seasoning, mainly because my mother did not use measuring spoons. She taught me how to make meringue pies two inches tall, and I had to beat the egg whites until they were stiff and then place them on top of the chocolate and lemon pies. Our eggbeater made a loud screeching noise when someone turned the handle to beat the egg whites. I loved helping my mother with the pies and my favorite ones were sweet potato, egg, custard, and pecan. Over the years, I gave my family the recipes for the cakes my mother taught me to bake.

When I was about 15 years old, my mother took me to work with her on Saturdays. After about a year of working with her, the lady next door asked if I could work for her. After six months, I told Mama that the lady had me doing a tremendous amount of work and only wanted to pay me a dollar. She said I could quit. The lady's house was in a gated complex with a security guard at the gate. I told her, "I am not returning to work for you; my mother needs my help."

She became upset and lied to my mother. She said I stole some of her jewelry and a coat. Then, she called the security guard to her home, and he pretended he was a police officer. He told me that the lady I worked for would have me arrested if I did not stay and work to pay for the stolen items. What a joke! I knew the guy was the security guard at the entrance gate. She wanted me to work for free.

After the performance, I told the lady, "I did not take anything from your home; I am going to my mother! You should be frightened of me because you could miss other items if I continued working!" That was the last time my feet entered her home.

My mother wanted her high school diploma; therefore, she went to Como High School to inquire about adult education. The school shared information about the adult G.E.D. classes held at Como Elementary. Students met in the building between the elementary and high school campuses at night. During the day, Carswell A.F.B. held an engineering class for Como students in the same building. Mama enrolled in the night classes and worked during the day. Mr. Clarence Russell, Mama's teacher, was accommodating and assisted her in all her studies until she graduated.

She then enrolled in a community night school for sewing, continued classes with the AA Allen ministry, and became a certified missionary. After she learned to sew, she made all of her dresses. Mama always wanted to go to college. Years later, one of her grandsons, Thomas Chadwick, in Houston, told Mama he had returned to Prairie View to finish college. Mama called his daddy, and said, "Frank, see if you can get me into Prairie View

College; I need to finish school." She purchased her first car, a 1953 Chevrolet, in 1960.

Mama loved children. After rearing her 12 children, a lady gave her baby to Mama. The child's name was Bip. After my mother raised Bip to age 12, Bip's mother returned and took her away. Mama felt devastated.

In 1967, the Queen of Sheba Grand Chapter, Order of the Eastern Star of Texas, Inc., bestowed her a membership certificate. It read: "This is to certify that sister Lula Mae Chadwick is a member of Lake Como Chapter No 297, O.E.S., located in Fort Worth, Texas. Therefore, we recommend that she be received and acknowledged by all true Masons and Eastern Stars wherever dispersed around the face of the globe."

Eight years after Deddy passed, another man, Barney Walton, arrived on the scene. We called him Brother Walton. He attended the community center in Dallas with my mother every day. Less than a year later, in June 1975, they married at the Fort Worth courthouse. Mama came home and simply announced, "Brother and I got married."

What a surprise! I asked my mother, "Why didn't you let us know?"

Mama said, "You would have told me, 'no.'"

Mr. Walton moved from his home in Dallas, to my mother's home in Lake Como. He had his own home and more property in Dallas, Texas.

I traveled from Stop Six to Como and frequently checked on Mama and Brother Walton during the week. They started depending on me for grocery shopping and other needs. After several years, traveling to Como to care for them became exhausting and difficult. After talking with Alvin in California, he purchased them a home in Stop Six near my house. I no longer had to drive from Stop Six to Lake Como weekly to care for them.

Alvin was a lifesaver; he didn't allow distance to keep him from participating in Mama's care. They both required additional care.

I had to get someone to come in and care for them while I was at work. Stacy Chadwick, my niece, agreed to help with their daily needs. Mama fussed at Stacy, her granddaughter, about sleeping with her husband, Brother Walton. Mama was in the beginning stages of dementia. She finally ran Stacy away.

Mr. Walton died on September 13, 1995. After Mama reached her late 80s, she became more dependent on us for care. Alzheimer's attacked her mental faculties. Oh, boy! Her actions made caregiving even more difficult for one person. I called Alvin about Mama's cognitive decline. He moved back to Texas and assisted me with her care. Alvin and both worked and couldn't stay home with her.

The family agreed to enroll Mama in an adult daycare center. Someone picked her up and transported her to the facility each day. Of course, she did not want to go, and every day, I had to drag her to the transportation bus that picked her up for daycare. When I took Mama outside to catch the bus, she would scream, "Call the law; she is trying to kill me!" She wore on my brain mentally, and I didn't know what else to do. I purchased a backpack, placed books inside it, and told her she was returning to school. That turned out to be a smart move on my part. After that, I never had any problem with getting her on the bus to the adult daycare center.

One day, she came home from the daycare center and would not talk or answer when we talked to her. Finally, when she spoke, her teeth fell out of her mouth. I asked her to open her mouth and discovered she had someone else's upper false teeth. Oh, Lord, what a sight to see! We called the center, and the nurse said another patient was missing her top denture plate. Two weeks later, the center called and told me my mother could not return after the end of the week. A patient had sat at the center's door, and Mama shoved him out the door; his wheelchair flew down the sidewalk.

Mama had two falls but she did not recuperate from the second one. They admitted her to the hospital and then transferred her to a rehabilitation center, however, her rehabilitation was unsuccessful. We then admitted her to a nursing center. That was the most difficult action for us to take. Her first Christmas in the nursing home was the most difficult. I rolled her around in the facility in her wheelchair and cried the entire time.

Alvin was there to assist her while she was in the nursing home. Because I was a registered nurse, Alvin would call on me to reprimand the staff when there was any problem with Mama's care. Finance was Alvin's responsibility. The team loved Alvin and did not care too much to see me coming. If Alvin could not visit, or if he went out of town, he called and told me to visit daily. The family celebrated Mama's birthdays in the nursing home each year while she was in the facility.

One of my sweetest memories of my mother was celebrating our birthdays. Every one of Mama's children enjoyed their special day. She entered the room and sang, "Happy Birthday to Chris, Happy Birthday to you!" Then, the whole family would chime in and sing the song. Not a birthday passed that Mama did not have a beautifully decorated cake waiting for the party. We might not have had ice cream, but we had much love and a giant cake to share with all. Celebrating birthdays for each family member continues today.

While in the facility, Mama met a young man, a housekeeper who looked just like Deddy. She loved for him to come to her room. She excitedly called out his name, "Hi Tucker!" Unfortunately, after four years in the facility, I received the dreaded call that Mama had died. She lived 94 years. My parents had 13 granddaughters and 17 grandsons.

Seated from left to right are the granddaughters and great-granddaughters of Dock Tucker and Lula Mae Woods Chadwick: Nilliah Jovan Chadwick, daughter of Edward Thomas Chadwick, Stacy Chadwick Nickerson, daughter of Howard Rosco Chadwick, sister-in-law, Bertha Chadwick, great-granddaughter, Nilliah Lauren Chadwick, daughter of Edward Thomas Chadwick, and granddaughter, Sharlene Chadwick, daughter of Donald L Chadwick, with her daughter Dezerae Valley. Also in the back row are granddaughters Neloise Chadwick Hollie, Debbie Chadwick, Carolyn Edwards Bullock, daughter of Virginia Chadwick Edwards, and Kimberlen Simpson Moss, daughter of Christene Chadwick Moss, great-granddaughters, Micaela Herndon, Micahella Titus Terrell, Lisa Edwards and Jorgette Louise Simpson.

Granddaughter of Dock Tucker and Lula Mae Woods Chadwick; Linda Chadwick Sands, daughter of Howard Rosco Chadwick.

Granddaughter of Dock Tucker and Lula Mae Chadwick; Cynthia Chadwick Antoine, daughter of Frank Thomas Chadwick.

Granddaughter of Dock Tucker and Lula Mae Chadwick; Tonja Chadwick, daughter of Bruce Harold Chadwick Sr. (Personal collection of Tonja Chadwick)

Grandsons of Dock Tucker and Lula Mae Chadwick.
Left to right: Kevin Adolphus Chadwick, Keith Eugene Chadwick, Douglas Chadwick, and Reginald Chadwick, sons of Adolphus Chadwick. (Personal collection of Kevin Adolphus Chadwick)

Front row: left to right: Steve Davis Jr., E. T. Chadwick Jr., Franklin Moss Jr., Keith Chadwick, and Edmond Moss. Back row: Steve Davis Sr., Courtney Chadwick, Bruce Chadwick Jr., and Jehrime Chadwick.

Grandson of Dock Tucker and Lula Mae Chadwick: Douglas Edwards, son of Virginia Chadwick Edwards.

Grandson of Dock Tucker and Lula Mae Chadwick, Thomas G Chadwick, son of Frank Thomas Chadwick.

The grandchildren of Dock Tucker and Lula Mae Chadwick. Left to right: Steve Davis, Ella Davis Myers, Harold Davis, Dorothy Lee Davis Titus, and Carlee Davis Jr. Children of Aldotsie Chadwick Davis. (Personal collection of Harold Davis)

My first cousins, Patricia Woods Alonzo, me, and Benniie Woods Allen, daughter of my uncle, Luke Woods. They surprised me with their presence at my retirement party.

CHAPTER SIX

Entering Womanhood

My aging mother called it, "A Rear-View Mirror Review." It was also called "Climbing Fool's Hill." It was a maturing stage: innocence, discovery, inquisitiveness, disobedience, guilt, confession, truths, and consequence. I've experienced them all. We're sliding back to how it all began.

Focusing on my studies during my school years was my challenge. It seemed like everyone expected me to do good. There were As all over my report cards. The teachers at Como High School were caring towards their students. One of them, Mrs. Mary Grigsby, was particularly supportive. She always offered advice on how to behave and not behave as a teenage girl. Her favorite topic to discuss was how girls should conduct themselves, carry themselves, and love themselves. Mrs. Grigsby consistently showed a caring attitude towards her students. She had a soft voice, wore heavy makeup and red hair, and was never without sunglasses. She spoke with me about my potential and how I had a unique skill for learning my subjects. Mrs. Grigsby also advised me to avoid getting involved with boys at my age. However, growing up and watching how my parents lived, instilled in me the awareness that my body belonged to me and me alone. I promised myself I would never allow a man to abuse or misuse me; I was too good for that.

In the spring semester of 1960, I was a junior in high school, and my friend, Charles Lorance Darden, was a senior, who would

My high school teacher/mentor, Ms. Mary Grigsby during the naming of Christene Chadwick Moss Elementary school.

would graduate in May. One day, he walked me home from school and no one else was there. Mama was attending a church conference in Houston, Texas.

My father had told me to tell Charles to stop walking me home. I didn't listen. On this day, he talked me into letting him into the house. Then, he talked me into sleeping with him. My mama did not advocate for, or teach me about birth control. All she taught me about birth control was to keep my dress down, my legs crossed, and my drawers up. That day, I was disobedient and got into more trouble than a little bit. I'd thought, *this one time, no one would know.* Boy was I wrong!

I did not tell anyone what happened. I was as quiet as a church mouse. Eventually, I shared the secret with Len Etta, who lived across the street. We walked to school together every day. I soon discovered that being pregnant was something I could not hide for long. I weighed 105 pounds and was healthy as a horse. My mother gave me Morgan David wine three times a week and Geritol daily for anemia. Well, "Church mouse Chris" started being nauseous in the morning but kept trying to fake the feeling by eating crackers. Mama entered the kitchen one morning and point-blank asked, "Chris, are you pregnant?"

How could Mama know? I thought. She must have been communicating with Jesus. Our Sunday School teacher told us Jesus was everywhere, and He could see everything we did. Surely, Jesus could not see in my belly. This teacher always said, "What you do in the dark will come to the light." Mama asked me a second time. Then, she said, "I know that look! I have had twelve babies. You have been with that boy."

I broke down and cried. My secret was no longer hush-hush; it was out! My dad knew. My father chimed in immediately and said, "I told that damn boy to keep his ass away from this house. Lula, the boy will have to marry this girl!"

My family had eagerly awaited my graduation from high school in May 1961. My mother shocked everyone when she announced I was pregnant and was getting married. In June of 1960, Charles and his family hurriedly planned the wedding at their home. When I threw my bouquet, Ella, my niece, tried to catch it and missed. The girl in front of her caught the flowers. However, Ella ran the girl down and took the flowers from her.

After our wedding, Charles immediately enlisted in the United States Air Force. He transferred to Roswell Air Force Base in New Mexico after basic training. I lived with my parents. When I got pregnant, I thought my mother would drastically chastise me. Back then, I looked like a lost sheep; I wore a two-piece tunic pregnancy outfit, a pair of black worn-down shoes, and a little ponytail. It shamed me to be pregnant before I finished high school. Honestly, I was scared of being pregnant. What do I do with a baby? I was going to hell, and of course, my mother had already told me I would take care of it myself because I had disobeyed God and my parents. Oh boy, no one knew the emotions that came over me. No one knew the angst I felt to be responsible for a child, when I was a child. I knew I had done wrong, and I believed God had punished me.

This is how I looked being pregnant in the 11th grade.

According to the Bible, God would punish you if you did not obey your parents. Being pregnant was my punishment. While in that state, I had time to think about my mistakes. Today, when I think about the incident, I have no regrets because of the beautiful children that came from it. Mama had made my dress for a musical recital in August 1956. I wore the same dress when I got married to Charles. Of course, I did not realize the hardship my pregnancy caused my mother. She probably wondered why I got pregnant after all the Bible teachings she shared with me. And I regretted having caused my parents shame and hurt, knowing they taught me right from wrong. They sacrificed many hours to act as babysitters for me while I finished high school. It was difficult to see how one act of disobedience would affect so many others.

Our baby boy, Edmond Lorance Darden, bounced in on January 7, 1961. After his birth, Mama took a bedsheet and made a binder. She wrapped my stomach tight for two weeks. Girdles were not available during that time. She instructed me to walk around the house seven times each morning for two weeks. She said this would help me return my womb to a youthful shape and I would not have baby fat. Unbelievably, it worked. After six weeks, my stomach was smooth and flat without stretch marks.

My first trip traveling alone was terrifying. When Edmond was three months old, I traveled by bus to join Charles at Roswell. Before I left for my trip to New Mexico, Mama gave me the following rules about discrimination and segregation as she prepared me for my trip:

- Do not talk to strangers; find a person, and always try to stay in their sight.
- Only drink out of the water fountain with "Colored" marked on it.
- Only use the bathroom that states "For Colored Only."
- Sit in the back of the bus.
- If someone makes ugly statements to you or calls you a nigger, ignore them.
- Keep the baby as quiet as possible.

Breastfeeding was my choice for giving Edmond nutrition. Doctor Carswell told my mother to bind my breasts to prevent milk from coming down, and help me dry my breasts after reaching the base. The binder was so tight I could hardly breathe; it felt like my breasts were in a girdle.

Mama prepared my meals and put them in a paper bag for the twelve-hour trip. Moving to Roswell Air Force Base was my first time away from the black community, and in no time, I encountered racism in the worst way possible. The bus stopped in a small town for a bathroom break and food. My mother reminded me before I left, that I could not go through the front door of a white business; to always go to the back door. I got off the bus with my baby to heat his bottle. This place had no back door, and we had to go to the rear window. I asked the lady there if she would heat my baby's bottle.

The lady responded, "We do not provide that service."

I asked her if she would place a pan of hot water in the window, and I would do it myself. In a nasty voice, she told me to leave the window. A little old black lady who rode on the same bus also stood at the window. She saw I was having a problem and said, "Go back to the bus, baby, and I will warm your baby's milk." When I got off the bus, I was already frightened. Now, my body shook, and I couldn't move my feet. I did not know how she could warm my baby's milk on the bus.

Once I returned to the bus, the lady with gray hair told me, "When a white person tells you to leave, baby, leave immediately. Sometimes, when you hang around, they will call the law and make up a lie that you did something wrong. The law will put you in jail in these little redneck towns. White people do not care about a black baby," she said.

Then, she shared with me her story about when she had to work in the fields. According to her, she and her husband lived on a farm with a white family in the 1940s. The people she worked for did not pay her to pick and chop cotton. She saw workers beaten, shot, and put out in the barn for days without food. Their children were not with them; they had sent them to live with her sister in California years earlier. She said, "Do you realize slaves have only been free for ninety years, and the white people hate black people? It's bad in the South." She told me, "My husband would not leave the white folks for whom he worked. He died, and I am getting my tail out of the South. I'm going to California. Baby, this is the Civil Rights Movement, and everyone is acting strange." She then said, "Be careful, stay safe, and stay on the bus until you reach your destination."

I knew nothing about the towns we were traveling through. It was cold in March. The lady asked me if I had a baby blanket. She took the blanket and wrapped it around my waist, then inserted the bottles against the skin of my body. My body heat warmed the milk. I thanked her, and I realized that our seniors went through many trials and knew how to make do in times of need. After that, I stayed on the bus until I arrived at Roswell.

I grew up in an all-black community, attended an all-black school, and came from an all-black family surrounded by blacks. I had no regular exposure to other ethnic groups. Once I arrived in Roswell, my new life began. Here I was, married and caring for a three-month-old baby with no experience. I knew nothing about being a wife, let alone a mother. By the grace of God, I made it through the summer. Edmond learned to love eggs and Cream of Wheat; they were simple to prepare. My mother had taught me how to cook and I remembered her lessons.

Charles and I joined other black couples on the base every weekend to play cards, drink, and smoke. The army wives cooked covered dishes for the gathering. Partying every weekend was not something I was accustomed to. I met many families and their children while living on the base. The ladies played Pokeno every weekend with pennies. It was like playing Bingo. We had game cards and chips. One person called out the alphabet with a deck of cards and we covered our numbers. Instead of saying, "Bingo!" we would yell, "Pokeno!" and someone would win the pot of money.

After being there a couple of months, I thought, *how does a person drink that much alcohol, still play games, and stand on their feet to go home?* I asked myself, *Is this all I have to look forward to?* Later, I thought, *Military service is not an ordinary event. One's life is on the line, and often, the family is left behind to live while you are away from home serving your country.* Often, one cannot see the stress that soldiers and their wives encounter. The soldiers drank and smoked to relax and try to maintain their sanity. I bought my own Pokeno set. Today, I play Pokeno with my nieces and friends during our many women's night out events. However, I soon learned that being away from home was less glamorous than I had pictured it.

My family and I were adamant about me getting my high school diploma. Mossey, wanted me to attend medical school. I felt I had already let her down, so not graduating was not an option. In

September, Charles took me to register at Roswell High School for the fall semester. It would be a breeze because it was only for one year. The first day of school was like a scene from a horror movie. While moving between classes, I only counted about 25 black students the entire day. The environment and culture were quite different. I had moved from an all-black school into a primarily white school.

There were 900 seniors. I told my husband I could have a good relationship with anyone for a year; I had to get my diploma. Yet, the teacher would not permit me to leave class or go to the bathroom. I could distinguish a difference in the treatment of students in her tone of voice and attitude. There was no talk of equity back then. My typing teacher placed me on a typewriter that was out-of-order most of the time. I told her I could type 60 words a minute. That's what I did in the 11th grade at Como High School.

Going to school while trying to care for my baby and a home became more than I could mentally handle. One morning, when I awakened Edmond, his body was hot as a firecracker. There was no thermometer to take his temperature. Charles took off duty and took us to the base doctor, who sent me home with medicine. I broke down, cried, and called my mother. "I am a baby trying to take care of my baby and I don't know what to do!" There was no manual for teenagers caring for babies. Mama told me to bring Edmond home; however, I didn't have money for the trip.

Mossey was a student in her last month of medical school in St. Paul, Minnesota. She called me and told me to pack the baby's clothes and bottles, and she would pick him up at the train station. She told me the exact location and time to meet her.

That following Friday morning, she arrived in New Mexico on the train. While the passengers boarded the train, she gave me a quick hug. She took Edmond, his bottles, and his suitcase, re-boarded the train, and continued traveling to Texas. Mama called me later and told me that little Edmond had arrived safely, and he was teething.

I asked, "How can the baby be teething?" He did not have any teeth.

She said, "I will explain later."

Mossey then traveled back to St. Paul. With my baby in Texas, I was ready to study and fulfill my school classes. My teacher was hateful to me. I do not know why this happened, but it started during my first month. I always carried extra pads in my purse when I had my period. After Edmond's birth, my period came like a rolling river. Some months, it would be so heavy that staying dry seemed impossible. It came while I sat in class. I asked the teacher to excuse me; I needed to go to the restroom. She said, "No, you may not leave the classroom." I explained to her I had started on my monthly. She told me to return to my seat, sit down, and then she pointed toward my seat. I returned to my seat and sat on my leg, not my dress, to prevent my clothes from getting soiled.

In less than five minutes, I felt the blood starting to stream down. The teacher stood in the doorway with her arm extended across the threshold when I walked to the door and requested to leave. When the teacher said, "No," I went under her arm and to the restroom. As I entered the restroom, blood trickled down my legs. Therefore, I went to a stall, sat on the toilet, took the wad of paper towels, and wiped myself off.

As I sat on the toilet, I recalled seeing white girls leave the classroom and go to the restroom without begging. I moved to another stall to clean myself and put on two fresh heavy-duty v-pads. The next day, I returned to class without saying a word. This was a true lesson in what discrimination meant. It was more than the teachings from my mother; it was an experience I will never forget because it became real to me. Therefore, I got the treatment of a "nigger." That semester at Roswell High School taught me more about discrimination than Mama could have ever told me. You might not have been called a "nigger" frequently, but only referred to as "That nigger." The word for them was just another word for being called "black." I was on display.

At the end of the fall semester, the school told me I could not graduate in May. The principal sent me a letter stating that the Roswell High School graduation requirements needed to be completed. It was too late to remove my picture from the yearbook or get my money back for the book. The first thing that came to my mind was to call Mama. I informed her that the school said I could not graduate in May. She said, "Some teachers and students think black students have no right to a quality education." She ordered me to pack my bags and tell Charles I was returning home to graduate.

I did what she said. "Mama told me to pack my bags and return home to graduate," I said to Charles.

Well, as usual, there was no money to go home. Mama had Mossey send me money to purchase a bus ticket. I could always depend on my sister to have my back. My eyes always "tear up" when I think of my life in Roswell and how Mossey wanted me to graduate and attend college.

I bought a ticket home, hopped on the bus, and decided not to get off until I saw the Fort Worth, Texas, sign. Lord, I was happy to get back home! My family was such a godsend. My mom, dad, and Donald L and Alvin were my lifesavers. I enrolled in Como High School for the spring semester and attended school every day, and the graduating class of 1962 placed my name on the roster for May's graduation. When I returned to Como, the first person I encountered was Mrs. Grisgby, my former teacher and mentor. She expressed immense joy in seeing me back for the graduation ceremony. Her encouraging words left an indelible impression on me, and instilled a belief that I could succeed and be whoever I wished to be. She advised me "to keep my chin up and persevere."

Charles came home to Texas to visit for Christmas 1962 to see us. Surprise, nine months later, in September 1963, I had my second child, Kim Camelia Darden. After Kim was born, I told my family my goal was to attend nursing school. My dilemma was that I did not know how to enroll in a nursing school. After Kim's birth, Charles was transferred to Montana Air Force Base.

I had not heard from Charles or seen him for a year. I had yet to learn when he completed his tour of duty in the Air Force or where he was living. A telephone call from a bill collector, told me he had left Montana with a woman. The bill collector called because my name was on a purchase concerning furniture. I told the bill collector I had never lived in Montana and not to call me back.

A year later, I visited my mother-in-law's home to watch the Fourth of July parade. I went inside to use the bathroom and walked along a path that led through the bedroom. By chance, I saw a letter from Charles on the dresser. He was now in California. My eyes lit up when I saw the letter. No one was watching, so I took the letter to the bathroom and read it. Before I returned to the parade, I replaced the letter on the dresser and mentioned nothing about it.

My mind floated back to when I was pregnant with Kim. I allowed the devil to convince me I no longer needed God or church. In my mind, I said, *I am not going to church anymore.* My church friend, Annie Pearl, and I went to the Airby club near Stop-Six, off Rosedale Street, to dance on the weekends; we didn't consider the danger of traveling late at night. We were always together and often caught rides with strangers.

One night, after dancing, we caught a ride to the Glass Key, a hole-in-the wall club, to grab a chicken basket. Almost everyone ate at either the Glass Key or Good Luck drive-in after the dances, usually around 1 a.m. or 2 a.m. While we ate and listened to music, we heard a loud commotion at the front of the club and someone yelled, "He has a gun!"

As a result, people panicked, ran, screamed, and fell over each other, as they headed towards the front door. I saw a big man with a sawed-off shotgun as he rushed toward the crowd. Terrified, I grabbed Annie Pearl's hand and we ran in the opposite direction.

I yelled, "Let's go through the kitchen. Leave the food!" We escaped through the back door and Annie Pearl cried.

As we ran, I prayed, "Lord, if you get me home safely tonight, I will never go to a bar or hole-in-the-wall again." And I kept my word. The following Sunday, I went to church, and from then on, the Sabbath became God's Day for me. I left behind all the devil's temptations. Annie Pearl later married an airman and moved away. Nowadays, I only dance when invited to a party, at home, or at a ball.

Charles and I divorced on December 8, 1966. We never lived together for more than a year; he lived in another state. I thought our marriage might have worked if he left military service. He finally returned to Fort Worth and lived with his mother in her home.

We remarried on August 4, 1967, and he moved into my home at 5645 Ramey Ave. After only a couple of months, our marriage started sliding downhill again. When Charles was at work, a woman called the house. Our relationship never improved.

One day, Charles came home unexpectedly and said he learned I had been dating someone while he was away in service.

I responded, "Sure! When the Air Force discharged you, you left Montana with a woman and never called home."

I also told him that he had been missing in action for over a year. I discovered he had lived in California; therefore, he could not tell me what to do. My last words to him were, "You left me for another woman." That day was not the time to try me.

My parents had already raised me. His threats were not okay. Not today. We argued, and he hit me and threw me on the bed. He thought he was going to beat me. I was a solidly built Geritol girl with a petite body, and not afraid of no one. I rolled off the other side of the bed, and we went to fist city. Yet, I do not know who won that battle; perhaps it was a draw. However, he got his coat and left for work. Charles looked distraught to hear I had not spent my days sitting in Como waiting for his return.

The same lady called and asked for him. I asked her, "Why do you keep calling my home? Charles is *married!*"

She said Charles gave her the number to call. "Make room for his black ass, and I'll send him to you. You can have him," I said.

When Charles returned home from work that night, I had all his belongings at the door and told him to leave. "The 'B' that keeps calling me is waiting for you." He left. I would have sent a "thank you card" if I'd known the lady who kept him from returning home when he left Montana. That was the best thing that could have happened to me.

Remarrying Charles was a mistake. I felt stupid filing for a divorce from the same man a second time, but I couldn't prevent it. A joyful day for me was November 14, 1968, when my divorce papers arrived. After my divorce, I needed money. I continued to file against him for the $25.00 per week of child support for our two children. However, Charles would not pay child support. It was more of a burden for me to miss work and go to the courthouse to file for child support. After a while, I started working and didn't need child support. I became independent and relied on my income to care for my children.

A word of advice: Ladies, when a man leaves you for another woman, count it as a blessing from God. Marrying the same guy twice doesn't work out most of the time. Moving on with your life might be in your best interest. Don't be afraid to develop confidence in yourself, build your career, and be an independent woman. Lastly, ask God for His guidance and never, under any circumstance, allow a man to use you as a punching bag; your parents have already reared you.

CHAPTER SEVEN

Nursing is It

My sister, Mary Virginia Edwards, said, "You do not have a husband. If you are going to nursing school, you must stop having babies." She scheduled an appointment for me with her doctor in Dallas. Mary Virginia taught me about birth control and how to use it. Hat's off to my sister. She did an excellent job teaching me. I did not have another child for 18 years.

Earning money to take care of my children was priority one. I worked for a family in the afternoon from 3 p.m. to 7 p.m. During the day, the family's housekeeper cleaned the home from 8 a.m. to 3 p.m. When the family's children arrived home from school, I prepared snacks and waited for the nanny to come for the night. The nanny was often absent, so I had to remain at the house several times until after 7 p.m. until their father arrived home from work. I would then have a problem finding a ride home.

One night, my friends invited me to a Dallas Cowboys' game. I had never attended one and wanted to go. At the end of my shift, I changed clothes and was ready to go. When the clock struck 7 p.m., I glanced outside and saw my ride. My employer, Mrs. Marble, came to me and said, "Chris, the nanny is ill, and you must stay until my husband gets home."

I had talked with the day housekeeper several times and knew this lady was not ill. Speaking calmly, I explained to Mrs. Marble my plans for the evening, and I told her, "My ride is waiting outside. I cannot stay."

She spoke to me as though she owned me. "Well," she said, "They will have to wait; your job comes first."

I politely told her that my shift was over. With my bag in my hand, I told her I was leaving. You guessed it; no more job for me!

One of the ladies I rode to the game with, Margie Nell Fikes, was a nurse at St. Joseph Hospital. I told Margie that I wanted to become a nurse. She gave me her number and said, "Chris, call me tomorrow." By the way, what a game! The Cowboys won.

The following Monday, I contacted Margie about pursuing a career in nursing. She said, "Chris, all you have to do is take a test at the School of Nursing at St. Joseph." I was frightened; I could only imagine failing the test. Margie picked me up and took me to the hospital. I passed it. Finally, my dream was coming true. I enrolled in the Licensed Vocational Nursing School in February 1965. Back then, the hospital paid you to attend nursing school. I depended on my family again for babysitting. That year was hard for me after I started LVN school. I continued to go out with Margie Nell and her friends. Donald L was always available to babysit my children. The Sigma Chi Epsilon Club invited me to become a member. The club comprised about 25 women. We conducted events every quarter to support "healthy" causes. Our concerts, dances, and movies kept the members busy and entertained. Although we enjoyed life, we volunteered with charitable organizations, visited nursing homes, and delivered food to the sick, and shut-ins.

I kept up with my studies. My books were priority number one; partying was number two. Although I partied every week, graduating from nursing school was my goal. During this period, I thought I rarely had time for church.

Margie Nell often called and encouraged me, "Chris, you are almost over the hump and will graduate soon. Let's go have fun."

"Girl, I do not have any time or money," I often responded, and Margie and her friends would take me out.

I wanted to be a doctor. Mossey had instilled this goal, or being part of the medical field, in me. I struggled to become a nurse.

Martin Luther King Jr., once said, "If a man is called to be a street sweeper. He should sweep streets even as a Michelangelo painted, or Beethoven composed music or Shakespeare wrote poetry. He should sweep streets so well that all hosts of heaven and earth pause to say; Here lives a great sweeper who did his job well." I decided that I would be the best nurse that ever lived.

To become independent, I left my parents' home and moved to a small house in the 5900 block of Blackmore Street in Como. Donald L was a major help. He often called and asked, "Are you ready for me to pick up you and the children?" He provided most of the babysitting services.

After working as a nursing student for several months, I moved from Blackmore Street to the Stop-Six apartments on Alexander Street; they were cheap. I never missed a day in school because of my family's support. I purchased a used blue Volkswagen from a guy at the hospital. Although I could not drive the car, I took advantage of the opportunity because it only cost $350.00. The vehicle had a four-in-the-floor stick shift.

Margie called and said, "Chris, buy the car. My friend will teach you how to drive a stick shift."

Following my purchase, I received driving lessons from Margie's friend. The car got me from point A to point B most of the time. Other times, like when my car wasn't working properly, I rode the bus or Margie picked me up.

Each week, I packed up my children, their clothing and groceries, and took both to my parents' home in Como. Both of my children danced and screamed when I dropped them off. They ran and cried from the front door to the back door.

When I turned the corner, they ran to the side door, jumped up and down and shouted, "Mommy, Mommy, don't leave us!" I could see and hear them through the screen door. Every time it broke my heart to hear their voices as I drove away. It hurt me; I had no alternative but to keep going. I picked them up on my days off. They could hear my car as it came down the road; it had a rattle and a loud shake. By the time I parked the car, they were laughing, and smiling. They would say, "Mama! Mama! We are ready to go home."

Donald L was good at playing with them and keeping them busy. He said, "Edmond and Kim stopped crying when your car was out of sight." My children did not understand that I could not provide for them without an education. School was the key to our independence. It was unfair for my parents to care for them; they also had no money. Still, Deddy always listened for the ice cream man's truck to purchase a treat for them.

Grandchildren of Dock Tucker and Lula Mae Chadwick. My brother, Alvin, helped Mama take care of his nieces and nephew. In the back row, from left to right: Debbie Chadwick, Edmond Darden, and Brenda Houston. In the front row, from left to right: Kimberlen Darden and Linda Chadwick.

While in school, I never worried about the care and safety of my children. My former mother-in-law, former sister-in-law, "Doll" Joyce Darden and niece, "Ketha" Chaketha Darden, kept my children fed, cared for, and entertained. My former mother-in-law often called and said, "Chris bring Edmond and Kim by; we will keep them tomorrow." She and her family always treated my children and me, unconditionally. I am grateful to Doll and Ketha; they were lifesavers. They often said they did not need combs or hair grease. They would tell me to leave them long enough to get Kim's hair washed and combed. They combed Kim's hair every week. I did not learn how to plait hair and Mama never took time to comb Kim's hair.

However, my mother and former mother-in-law disagreed over taking care of my children. She offered to keep the children once a week to give my mother a break. However, when I left my children with her, my mother would wait until Doll had combed Kim's hair, then she would drive by and scoop them out of my former mother-in-law's yard. Edmond, said, "When my cousins saw Mama Lula coming, they yelled, 'Here comes Mrs. Chadwick!'"

They tried to hide; it was too late. Mama would drive by the house, open the car's back door, and yell, "Y'all get in this car!"

She would then take off flying down the road. Frustrated, my former mother-in-law would call and say, "Chris, your mother just came by here and took the children out of the yard!"

"I will talk to Mama," would be my reply. Unfortunately, talking to her did not help. She didn't want to share my children. The year was challenging for me because of nursing school and being a peacekeeper between my mother and my former in-laws.

When I was a child, I suffered from gum disease, which caused many of my teeth to decay. As a result, I had rotten teeth and cavities across the front of my mouth. As a grownup, I had my teeth replaced by a skilled dentist whom I chose. The process took over three months, but I attended nursing school every day without fail. However, my face remained puffy and swollen for four months.

Finally, my dentist inserted my dentures, and I have worn them ever since.

The last hurdle I had to cross to get my nursing license was the state examination in Austin. "Hallelujah!" I passed the test for LVN with excellence and graduated in February 1966. The hospital hired me full-time after I received my license. I wonder how my brain kept all the knowledge required to graduate. Hospital classes started at 8 a.m. and many days, I arrived home at 4 a.m., just in time to shower and get my books. As long as my car started, I then quickly drove to St. Joseph Hospital.

Living in the Stop Six apartments exposed me and my children to many adverse events. It was quite a challenge. Men loitered around the entrance. Food was constantly on the hallways and stairs instead of in the trash. Living on the second floor was especially difficult for me, because the people sitting on the stairs would usually refuse to budge, and that created significant obstacles to navigate around. The noise level skyrocketed on Saturday nights, thanks to the constant knocking on doors. This lifestyle was for someone else.

After I graduated and started my actual job, I moved out of the apartments and into a rented house on Carol Avenue off Miller Avenue. Shortly afterward, my realtor located a house at 5645 Ramey Ave. I bought it. It was directly across the street from Dunbar High School. Owning my home was a dream. I grew up in a house and did not want anything less for my children. My neighbors were excited and helpful.

Unbelievably, I know better than anyone that God played a significant role in my life. He blessed me with a supportive family and neighbors. The Washington family lived on my left, and Betty Forte lived on my right. Our family was such a close-knit family, when I needed something, they were always nearby. Since Bruce had his own upholstery shop, he found old furniture on the side of the road, rebuilt it and upholstered it for my new home. During nursing school time, I often struggled to make ends meet. There were many instances when I couldn't afford to buy food for myself and instead spent my money on groceries for my mother, who took care of my children. I was never a big eater and could quickly get by on tuna fish sandwiches and pinto beans. I also knew how to make cornbread.

When my car didn't work, I took the bus to the hospital for school and to my mother's house. Sometimes, I would get off the bus at my mother-in-law's house, and my mother would pick me up with my children. However, the bus stop to my mother's house was quite far and was a long walk. But I made it.

Edmond attended Little Tommy Tucker private school in kindergarten and first grade. From private school, I enrolled him in the neighborhood school, Rosedale Park Elementary. Kim attended Blanche's School in Stop Six and then transferred to Little Tommy Tucker in first grade. For the second grade she enrolled in the neighborhood school, Rosedale Park Elementary. In third and fourth grade, Kim attended Eastern Hills Elementary.

Edmond and Kim eagerly looked forward to their yearly birthday celebrations when they were in elementary school. Our home served as the party palace for their birthday parties, and their nearby cousins would also join in. Large groups of children would play in the yard and all around the house, and make it an enjoyable time. The grandparents enjoyed these parties, too.

Nowadays, parents spend a lot of money on entertaining their children during their birthday parties. Children request to celebrate birthdays at fancy venues, such as golf courses, rocket ships, Chuck-E-cheese, skating rinks, and many other places. We made do with the items I could squeeze from my grocery list.

Edmond and Kim with their cousins at one of his birthday parties.

One day during our weekly family talks, my children came into my room with a new idea. Edmond said, "Kim and I decided that every Friday night would be our drive-in movie night." They loved going to the movies during the summer months. I purchased little cups of mosquito deterrents and spray for our comfort. We drove into the drive-in, placed the speaker in our car window, and the night was on. They always liked the homemade hot dogs, popcorn, and drinks I prepared. We could not afford to purchase those items at the movies. We looked forward to Friday night entertainment with excitement. That special night was a lot of fun.

In 1967, when my father died, my neighbors encouraged me to continue my education. Tarrant County Junior College opened in 1967. I applied to the Registered Nurses Program and they approved my application. It was excellent. Because I never lived on campus, I had yet to learn what college life was actually like. I studied hard to be successful. I was one of only two black students admitted into the program. Mrs. Gipson and I helped each other because we did not want to fail. I took 18 hours a semester, year-round, for two years.

My acceptance into the first Tarrant County College Registered Nurse program came at a joyous time. The campus had a large enrollment of primarily young people, ages 18 to 20 years old. There were several more students in my age range. Attending college reminded me of the semester I spent at Roswell High School. There was much racial division. Once I learned the culture of the nurse's program, things fell into place.

My years of growing up and observing my parents deal with racist attitudes built my resilience toward surviving the racist attitudes in class during our hospital training settings, and even in patients' rooms while training. My mother also told me, "Chris, if they do not touch you, just keep walking. Do not engage in conversation when you hear the word, nigger!" Sometimes patients did not want me to be in the room during the training period. That was okay; I practiced enough to receive my grade for observations.

The TCC nursing program was the first; all the books were new, and my mother often said, "These books cost a pretty penny." Now, was a time when I *could have* used hand-me-down books. I did not care about the previous owner. When we complained about the second-hand books that our school provided students in the second and third grade, we wanted new books. The white students had written all over the books before they were handed down to black schools. Because the two of us black students did not have money, we chose a lab book to share. It was hard to do. If we wanted to pass the course, we needed the book and needed more money to purchase it . The most annoying thing for me was when I asked a student a question in class. The student would act as though she did not know or did not hear me. However, she answered the question when asked by the instructor. I realized this group would not help me with any academics. One student, Mrs. Diaz, loved to be around us. Mrs. Gipson and I collaborated and worked together. Nothing mattered but graduating.

However, in my last semester, I struggled with passing my college math class. My neighbor, Betty Forte, was the director of

Fort Worth Independent School District's mathematics department. I told her about the problem I had. She tutored me through my college math class, and I passed the course. I was on the Dean's List while a student at TCC.

I graduated from TCC-The Registered Nurse Program. From the front, I am sitting on the second row from the right, I am the second nurse.

"Hallelujah!" I reached my goal. Graduation day was May 1969. What a fantastic feeling! Walking across the stage to receive a diploma was indescribable. I wanted to shout on stage. All I could think of was, *I made it! Now, I can feed my children.* I passed the Registered Nurses exam in Austin and earned my R.N. license.

After completing my nursing education and getting my R.N. license, St. Joseph Hospital hired me to work the 11 p.m. to 7 a.m. shift in the Surgical Recovery and Intensive Care Unit. However, I found staying awake during the night shift challenging. Every night, between 2 a.m. and 3 a.m., my eyelids got heavy and droopy while taking pulses, or even while walking, no matter how much coffee I drank. Despite my request for a transfer to the day shift, the hospital refused to accommodate my needs. I later discovered that the hospital only hired new graduates who were black as RNs for the night shift and white RNs for the day shift.

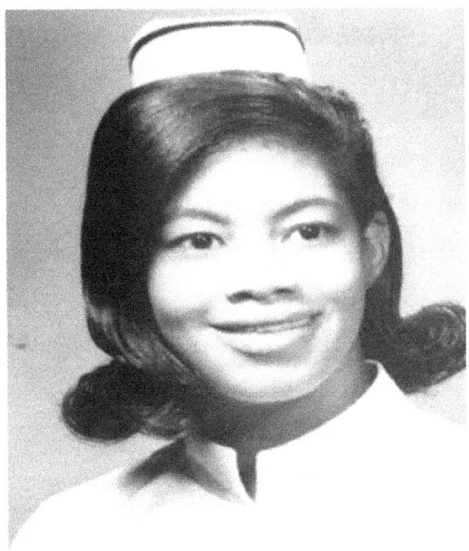

My prayer: "Thank you Jesus for keeping me focused on my goal!"
Now I can take care of my children.

In 1971, my luck changed. I received a call from the owner of Webber Nursing Center. The caller asked if I would schedule an interview for a Director of Nurses position at their new nursing facility in east Fort Worth. Long-term care was not on my list of places to work, so I did not answer the owner immediately. A couple of nights later, I was at work, and at about 2:30 a.m., I fell asleep and tumbled off my work stool. Guess what? I woke up immediately, embarrassed to be working the night shift. My actions were not acceptable to me. I told myself *patients deserved an alert nurse.* The same weekend, I was off duty. My children were in the kitchen while I lay on the bed, exhausted. I fell asleep and Kim walked into my bedroom with her body covered with flour. She was white as snow. Kim had poured flour over the kitchen floor, cabinets, and tabletops. What a sticky and messy situation. They giggled, and thought the incident was funny. When Kim took a step, flour fell off her clothing. What a sight to see. I dared not whip her.

I answered the Webber Nursing Center call and asked one question, "Is this position on the day shift?" The voice on the other line said "yes," and my answer was, "Yes, I will take the job." I had yet to learn what a nursing home job required.

Mr. and Mrs. J.W. Webber hired me as their director of nurses (D.O.N.) in 1971 in their newly built nursing home at 4900 East Berry. I opened the facility and never looked back. The credit goes to Patricia Hobson, RN, who operated their south side facilities, Patsy Dockery, my assistant director of nurses, and Lula Wattley, the housekeeping supervisor, who provided me with on-the-job training.

As the director of nurses in a long-term care facility, I ensured residents received quality nursing care. I maintained an open-door policy for team members, families, and residents. The nurse aide's job was the most critical in the facility, as the care provided by staff was essential to maintaining the residents' quality of life. Staff turnover could make it challenging to fully maintain the level of care needed to support residents. While training staff was critical, turnover was inevitable, and higher wages could help keep staff. Mr. Webber told me that raising staff salaries was not part of my job description, therefore, I left that topic alone.

This job was like returning to school for me. Heck, I did not care; working during the day was my immediate goal. The Federal and State regulations were available in my office, in two-inch-thick journals. During my tenure, one team member was consistently absent, did not complete the residents' assigned care, and was not in the facility when the nurse needed assistance with the residents. On weekends, the building always required more staff. After many infractions, I had to terminate nurse aides and continuously train inexperienced staff because of absenteeism. The team cooperated well with the residents, and the residents were happy.

We once admitted a new resident who continuously walked into the activity room. I stopped my work and went out to talk with him. When I approached him, he looked up at me with a smile and said, "Hello," then he threw a hot cup of coffee at me and all over my outfit. I was unaware of this resident's mental derangement when he was admitted. Mental health was an issue years ago and it still exists.

When patient care declined, the facility's odor became intolerable. My instincts told me to visit the 11 p.m. to 7 a.m. shift nurses to see if the facility should provide more resources. One night at about 2 a.m., the nurse called me at my home and said, "My nurse aides are asleep in the residents' rooms. Would you please come over to the facility?"

While investigating, with the assistance of the charge nurses, I found two team members sleeping in the patient rooms during their night shifts. My memory took me back to the time when I became sleepy while on duty. I left that job in order that patients would receive quality care while in the hospital. I immediately woke the nurse aides and said, "Please wake up ladies and go home to sleep!" I terminated their employment, as residents must receive the ultimate necessary care. While it was challenging to let go of several employees, I knew it was essential to maintain the level of care our patients deserved. The patients' care should always come first, and I did not tolerate team members who came to work only to get a paycheck.

After reviewing the residents' needs, I developed a nurse's aide class to teach them how to provide care to the senior citizens in the facility. While working as a Nursing Home D.O.N., I gained a reputation with the Texas Department of Aging and Disability Services as an outstanding L.T.C. nurse. The agency saw I believed in improving the quality of care of all nursing home residents. I knew all the State and Federal regulations, and the state department offered me a nursing surveyor position. However, I had my eyes set on returning to the hospital setting.

Working in the nursing home kept me extremely busy, and I hardly had time to care for my personal needs. Lucky for me, my sisters, Aldotsie and Virginia, owned separate beauty salons in Dallas, Texas. One or the other would always allow me to come to their beauty shop at 6 a.m. to get my hair and beauty treatments before other clients arrived. This arrangement saved me from taking time away from my stressful day at the nursing home. After two years of working in the facility, it received a Superior Rating from the Texas Department of Health during our annual inspection. Along with my photo, the nursing home recognition story ran in the *Fort Worth Star-Telegram*. This accomplishment kick-started my career in long-term care.

While working for the Webbers, I attended Nursing Home Administrator School at El Centro College in Dallas and received my N.H.A. license in 1972. The owners moved me to their son's facility. State Representative Bobby Webber owned the Eastwood Village Nursing Center and I became an administrator. The job was highly demanding, and I spent most of my daylight hours there.

This job was golden. What better way to enrich the lives of senior citizens in the nursing center? Being a champion for senior citizens allowed me to make a real difference in their lives. My goal was always to elevate a patient's quality of life. It was a rewarding opportunity. I want to thank Mr. J.W. and Mrs. Charlie Mae Webber for taking a chance on me when I knew nothing about long-term care. They allowed me to learn about leadership, business, and finances.

CHAPTER EIGHT

Husband Number Two

While working for the Webbers, I met a young man named Franklin Douglas Moss through my nursing friends, Gloria Roy, Ann Watkins, and their husbands, Tony Roy and Billy Watkins. They invited me to play cards. Little did I know they were setting me up on a blind date. During the card game, the group introduced me to this handsome guy. My eyes drifted toward him several times, and I caught him watching me. He talked throughout the evening. Each time I glanced at him, I could see more of his slim body, inviting smile, and charismatic charm. At that moment, I told myself, I need to know more about this man. I did not want to appear too eager. Frank casually asked for my phone number at the end of the evening and wanted to know if he could call me. I replied, "Yes, here is my number." My friends invited me back to play cards when I was off duty.

Waiting for the telephone call seemed like weeks. However, at the end of the week, I picked up the telephone, and Frank said, "Hello?" in a soothing, sexy voice. After a lengthy conversation, we both discussed receiving an invitation to the Christmas balls.

Every December, everyone in *Who's Who* awaited their invitation to attend the Ambassadors of Fort Worth Ball and the Fort Worth Assembly Ball. When I met Frank, we both had received an invitation to the Fort Worth Assembly Ball. In 1972, Frank and I agreed to meet there. The event was electrifying. Frank came to my table and asked me if I would like to dance. We started a conversation, and after that night, we started dating. It was love at first sight. We both loved this annual activity because everyone danced the night away. After the balls, we attended late-night parties.

Frank and me at the Ambassador's Ball.

Disappointment set in when I learned that Frank still lived with his parents. Frank was 29 years old, and I wondered if he would leave his parents to get married. The only financial responsibilities he had were his car note and his wardrobe. About three months after we started to date, Frank moved out of his parents' home and into an apartment.

Our friends, Gloria Roy, Ann Watkins, Billy Watkins, and Tony Roy, loved playing cards together on weekends. Time moved quickly; we both looked forward to visiting our friends. Frank worked in the planning department at Tarrant County.

He later became a member of the Ambassadors of Fort Worth, Inc. We were both involved in the church. I attended the Church of God in Christ, and Frank attended Ebenezer Missionary Baptist Church as a Sunday School teacher. After we started to date, I moved my membership to Ebenezer.

We dated for over seven months. While we dated, Frank had to comply with two rules. The first rule was that he could not stay overnight at my place. I had two children and did not want them to wake up and find a stranger in our home. The second rule; he must have his own automobile. I always used my car for work.

Eventually, Frank took me to meet his parents. During our conversation, Mrs. Moss said she was born February 9, 1915, in Cameron, Milam County, Texas. Her parents were Eddie Moten and Ella White-Moten, and she was the eldest of their two daughters and the third of four children of Eddie. She died on March 31, 2008.

Mr. Claudie Moss, Sr. told me he was born March 15, 1917, in Cox's Providence, Texas. His parents were Johnny and Mary Madison Moss. He was the fourth of five children. Mr. Moss attended school in Cameron, Texas, and he and his wife had two boys, Claudie Moss Jr., and John Moss. He moved his family to Fort Worth, Texas, in 1942 and they joined Ebenezer Missionary Baptist Church. They later had three more sons: Franklin Douglas Moss, James Moss, and Kenneth Moss. He died on May 30, 2007.

The family of Claudia Sr. and Eva Moten Moss. Front row seated, left to right: Claudia Jr., Franklin Sr., James Moss, Kenneth Moss and me. The row behind the brothers; Briijon, Clea, Carolyn holding the baby, Erika, Lisa, Donna, Angel, Sharon, Gabby, James Jr. behind Gabby, Wesley behind James Jr., Arthur next to Greta, Cameron, Claudie and Marquel is behind Clea. On floor; left to right, Julian, Jake, Elijah, and Franklin III.

Frank and I loved going to the theater to see plays while we dated. Occasionally, we watched a good movie. We enjoyed our friends and family. Our schedules were always full of events, including the Sigma Chi Epsilon Social Club, the Florence F. Brooks Club, and many community functions. I cooked for Frank; he always enjoyed coming over for dinner. It was during one of those dinners that he proposed to me. As we sat on the couch and watched television, Frank seized my hand and asked, "Will you be my wife?"

I said, "Yes," with no hesitation. Looking back, I realized that food played a significant role in our relationship.

Our wedding occurred on Saturday, June 9, 1973, at Ebenezer Missionary Baptist Church. Frank had never been married; this was my second marriage. Moss & Moss Interior Design, my sister-in-law's business, planned my wedding and reception. Janet Moss was one of the top wedding planners in Arlington, Texas. My wedding dress was cream satin with white embroidery lace trim. The neck was a Queen Elizabeth turtleneck designed as an 18th-century gown. The wedding included both of my children. Kim was the flower girl, and Edmond was the ring bearer, along with a younger neighbor, Keith Washington.

Getting married to Frank filled the air with excitement from my family and friends. Mama gave me an inspirational talk while we waited in the foyer for the wedding to start. She told me I had developed by attending school, having my children, and striving to be an exemplary mother. "Now," she said, "you will aim to be a good wife."

She gave me a flower and a kiss on the cheek, saying it was for good luck. Gwendolyn Washington, my next-door neighbor, was my maid of honor. Levi Davis was Frank's best man. My father was deceased, but my brother, Frank, gave me away. Frank and I married, and he graduated with a Master of Science degree in the Urban Studies Program at the University of Texas Arlington that same month. His professor, Dr. Paul Geisel, had planned his class trip, going to Mexico City, by train. Since Frank and I needed to review our financial status, we used this opportunity for our honeymoon.

Despite warnings from Frank's classmates to fly back home at the end of the trip, we returned on the train. Later, we found out why his classmates had warned us not to take the train.

When I told Frank when we were leaving, I said, "We should plan to travel back by plane with your classmates."

Frank immediately said, "Chris, let's just ride back on the train."

Hesitantly, I agreed. Little did I know Frank would be like this throughout our marriage. As a Virgo, he seldom took advice from anyone else. We rented a private car for our honeymoon and enjoyed the scenic journey through dry land, beautiful trees, and tumbleweed. In Cuernavaca, we took a bus to see the Pyramid of the Sun and the Pyramid of Mood, the giant pyramids in the country. We toured the Cuernavaca Cathedral the following day, which took up much of our time. After my shopping spree for wicker baskets, tequila glasses, teacups, and other trinkets, we returned to the train, which upset our honeymoon spirit. The air conditioner on the train did not work correctly, and this was in the hot month of June. The kitchen had no food, and the beer was hot. Our train ran six hours behind schedule. Finally, we left the train and caught the bus back to Fort Worth.

I was unaware that Frank's mother cooked dinner for her five sons and their families every Sunday. Frank invited me to his mother's house on the first Sunday after our wedding. The meal looked delicious, and Frank urged me to eat. Mrs. Moss invited me in and said, "Welcome to the table and come join us for dinner."

During my first visit to their home after our marriage, his parents sat in the living area while my two children and I joined them. The family conversation kept everyone engaged until Mrs. Moss blurted out, "I am not a babysitter."

I understood her point. With a reassuring smile, I said, "Do not worry about Edmond and Kim; I have never had to locate a babysitter." My mother and my former mother-in-law always called me to bring them to Como. I wanted to let her know that although I had two children coming into this marriage, I was an asset to her son and not a liability.

From that Sunday on, after church, the family went to her house for Sunday dinner. I always helped clean up after the meal and thanked her for her hospitality. Sometimes, her sons dropped food off at her home to help with her grocery bill.

During one of our Sunday dinners at Frank's mother's house, I disagreed with my husband about our wedding anniversary. Since then, Frank has not been cooperative regarding our anniversary.

After returning from church that day, Frank asked me, "What day is today?"

I answered, "I don't know." He immediately became angry and accused me of forgetting our anniversary.

I said, calmly, "Frank I have had an exhausting week and just forgot. I mentioned the anniversary last week!" I suggested that we still celebrate, but he declined, saying he wouldn't remind me of our anniversary in the future. He also added that it must not be important to me. Despite my efforts over the years, I have been unable to convince him to celebrate our wedding anniversary on July 9.

Once we got married, my life became fascinating and always busy. We lived in my home at 5645 Ramey Avenue for about one year. We purchased a beautiful 2,197 square foot home at 2848 Winterhaven Dr., Hurst, Texas, in Wintergreen Acres Estates. Dreaming of a large home during my childhood became a reality. We gladly said goodbye to the small one-bathroom house with only two bedrooms. Our new home had four bedrooms and two bathrooms with plenty of living space. The Mansfield Planning Department hired Frank as their director. Two years later, Mr. Pickalinski called Frank to come and work for the Council of Governments in Arlington, Texas. This job meant increased income.

Kim was not too fond of the idea of me marrying Frank. She even got her brother, Edmond, to write a letter to persuade me not to go through with it. When I asked her about the letter, Kim said, "I do not want Frank to take you away." She felt I was the only one who genuinely loved her, as her father did not care much. Kim also expressed her fear that if Frank took me away, no one would be left to love her.

I tried to reassure her and said, "Kim you are gaining a loving father who will love you and Edmond as much as I do." I do not know if this put her fears to rest.

After we married, she started inventing ideas to get our attention. One time, she even packed a bag to run away. Edmond followed her, and they both had filled a run-away sack and left the house while Frank and I watched TV. I must admit, I did not look for them right away. But when it started to get dark outside, they returned to the house. As it turned out, they had been hiding on the back patio the entire time. It was a beautiful fall day, and they had a fun time outside.

Another incident took place when we moved to Hurst. Kim was about ten and was sewing clothes for her doll one Saturday. She decided to take some stick pins from her sewing kit and put them in Frank's shoes. When Frank put one of his shoes on, he screamed out in pain. I immediately knew who did it. I called out, "Kim get in here. What have you done now?"

She knew the stunt was wrong. Frank said, "Kim never do that again." Kim told me later she thought Frank was going to whip her. After that stunt, Kim stopped the pranks.

In 1975, my work schedule became less demanding, so I took advantage of the opportunity to enroll in Texas Wesleyan College. My focus was on a degree in Sociology and Psychology. The college was near my home. Few blacks enrolled in TWC. My high school transcript and my application met the admission requirements. However, after enrolling at TWC, I had to adapt to the reality of college life and adjust my study habits accordingly. With time, my college plans and study habits became one, and my classes fell into place. During this time, I met Mr. Earl Brown, instructor of Sociology who improved my thinking skills and helped me plan to graduate. He gave me books and journals to read, which improved my skills for testing. The college had only one black professor on staff, and he did not teach the courses I needed to graduate. I remember the long hours of studying in the cold library, the large textbooks, staying awake at night cramming for tests. I kept my fingers crossed I would pass all my exams.

An exciting event occurred while attending TWC and working as a long-term care administrator. Dovie Webber entered me into a Ms. UNCF contest. I told Dovie I did not want to take part. She did not listen to me and entered my name into the competition. Frank remembers the event as a fundraiser. In 1975, Dovie raised the most money, and I won the crown as Ms. UNCF; there were also a second and third-place winner.

Wedding day June 9, 1973 – Mr. and Mrs. Franklin Douglas Moss.

On my wedding day, my mother gave me her blessings and she wore a dress she had made.

Frank and me on our honeymoon in Cuernavaca, Mexico.

I was crowned Ms. UNCF by Theresa Howell, First Vice President of Greater Fort Worth Area Negro Business and Professional Women's Club, Inc.

As I sat among the graduating class of 1977, I held back the tears, thinking about my struggle to get to that point in my life. When I reached for my Bachelor of Science diploma in Sociology from TWC, I could only scream, "Thank you, Jesus!"

Before meeting Frank, he and I both worked within our community. After we got married, I fully realized that Frank had an incredible commitment to various projects. One day, while living on Ramey Avenue, I asked Frank, for the third time, to cut the lawn, which had grown tall. I watched from the window as he rolled the lawnmower from under the carport. *Finally,* I thought *he will take care of it.* However, my relief was short-lived when Frank placed the lawnmower in the trunk of his car. "Where are you taking it?" I asked.

"To cut the grass at the church cemetery!" Frank responded. I soon realized that I was in trouble with getting him to complete household chores. His lack of attention to home chores became a recurring issue as our marriage progressed. I knew it was time to sit down and have a serious conversation with him about putting his family first. It was around this time that he traveled to Boston to attend Economic and Finance classes at Harvard University. I worried that the trouble at home would be an unwanted topic of conversation. However, while he was away, he wrote me a beautiful love letter and promised to work harder on his responsibilities at home.

By the Grace of God, we both had lucrative careers. We played cards with our friends and had many weekend parties. We both were involved in many organizations and activities. We were members of the F. Brooks and Gray Club and we modeled in its fashion shows. Frank was a member before we married. He helped organize the meetings and fashion reviews at the Blackstone Hotel in downtown Fort Worth. Mother Gray assigned me to teach the youth about etiquette, grooming, and respect for elders, teachers, and authority figures. The lesson covered grooming, hygiene, posture, and table manners. Two sisters operated this club. Mother

Gray was a sweet old lady who prepared dinner in her home for members after the fashion shows. Her sister, W.L. McClure, was a little more of a challenge. Mother Gray called her sister, McClure.

Jubilee Theatre was one of our favorite places to attend. It started with Rudy and Marian Eastman on June 19, 1981, at 1801 East Victory. After a year at that location, the board decided Jubilee Theatre would become a "gypsy theater." In 1983, Jubilee moved to 3114 Rosedale Street across from TWU. Jubilee conducted a capital campaign that resulted in the ability to move the theater to Fort Worth's Sundance Square at 506 Main Street. Their performances were like no other theaters' productions downtown. I enjoyed the musicals more than the plays. Many of the stories, told through the scripts, followed along with the southern theme of slavery. Frank and I always purchased a season ticket to ensure Jubilee reserved our seats for our dates. He was a member of the theater board and a friend of the founders.

When Frank married me, I was a package deal. I came with two children, but it didn't matter to him. I never doubted his commitment to fatherhood because he was a true father to my children. He treated them as though they were his own. We traveled and visited every museum in Texas and across the country. Whenever we took vacations or traveled for any reason, we took Edmond and Kim and Frank always drove. We always packed our walking shoes because Frank would find the museum for us to visit. It was usually an African American Museum. They looked forward to vacationing in Galveston and Corpus Christi, and staying at the Red-Carpet Hotel. The beach, swimming pool, walking tours, and eating out were unique activities for them. We always enjoyed ourselves on the trips.

CHAPTER NINE

Family Matters

Edmond was in the sixth grade, and Kim was in the fourth grade. Edmond attended Dunbar Middle School on Willie Street and Kim was in Eastern Hills Elementary School. We lived right on the line for desegregation, therefore, Kim had to leave Rosedale Park Elementary and attend Eastern Hills. Around this time, Frank and I made a unanimous decision to stop contacting my ex-husband, Charles, for child support. Rarely did he pay the $25.00 a week child support order and the children seldom heard from him.

We entertained ourselves in our home on most holidays. Over the years, we have filled our little black directory with numerous names of friends. Our home became the birthday party palace. God was good. Life was good. Once we moved to Hurst, Edmond and Kim attended school in a different district, Birdville ISD. We enrolled Edmond in Watauga Junior High School and Kim in Smithfield Elementary.

Edmond had an exciting middle school experience. It was his first time attending a desegregated school. Football became his passion, and he played football in the seventh and eight grades. Kim enjoyed her elementary school experience. She became an avid reader and carried her books to read wherever she traveled.

However, she could not understand why the white girls' hair continuously flowed down their backs. She would take her hair down at school to be like them. When Kim returned home in the afternoon, her hair would be all over her head, like a big Afro style.

She only realized her hair was different when Frank and I talked with her about skin color, culture, and hair texture.

After graduating from Watauga Junior High, Edmond attended Richland High School, where he played football. His PE class was gymnastics. Edmond excelled at gymnastics, and Coach Charles Cowan invited him to work out with the team, The Gyros. The Gyros competed against All-American and international teams.

In the eleventh grade, during one of his gymnastic practices, he broke his arm. This accident kept him out of the sport for several months.

Frank and I accompanied him to several gymnastic competitions, locally and abroad. When international teams traveled to America to compete, they lived with the host gymnast families, and it was the same when the team traveled abroad.

Coach Cowan invited us to attend the USA International Gymnastics competition in France. Although Frank was hesitant about the cost of the trip, I saw it as a once-in-a-lifetime opportunity. We went, and while there, we celebrated our wedding anniversary. We flew into Paris, France. From there, we boarded our tour bus and our activities began. We went to Amsterdam, Belgium, and London, England.

During our stay, we took a tour of Paris and visited famous landmarks such as the Notre Dame Cathedral, the Eiffel Tower, Anne Frank's home, and Buckingham Palace. At the palace, we witnessed the changing of the guard, and saw the gold iron fence with the guards in formation in red and black uniforms sitting tall on black horses.

Frank and me visiting the Eiffel Tower.

Enjoying a picnic with families in France.

Edmond, touring before a gymnastic performance.

The families of the abroad gymnastics team took us on a sightseeing tour, picnics and other events held for the USA families. Watching him compete on the pommel horse and the gymnastics team compete against other countries filled us with thrill. The gymnastics team's performance left us in awe.

While we traveled, Kim stayed with Adolphus and Gwendolyn. Kim attended Smithfield Jr. High School after completing elementary school, and that's when she noticed the treatment of blacks was different. Unfortunately, she experienced discrimination in school early on for the first time in Birdville School District. When Frank and I attended an event, the school officials did not know our children's last name was Darden; they didn't know they belonged to the Moss family. This bothered the children.

One Saturday in November, I was in the shower mid-morning when I almost passed out. I screamed out to Edmond and Kim. They could barely get me to bed because of the sharp pains in my abdomen. Edmond called 911, and the paramedics came and transported me to the hospital. According to my x-rays, the doctor told me a tubal pregnancy had developed in my right ovary. The ovary burst, causing excruciating pain, and as a result, the doctor removed my right ovary. The doctor did not release me from the hospital until the week before Thanksgiving. Frank prepared a delicious Thanksgiving dinner for us.

An article in a 1975 newspaper congratulated Frank on his new position as Mansfield, Texas City Planner. Dr. Gwendolyn Morrison called my husband and asked if he had a wife interested in joining a service organization. Frank provided all my information to Dr. Morrison; I became aware later that she was creating a new organization and wanted me to be a charter member. Today, I am a charter member of the Greater Fort Worth Area Negro Business and Professional Women's Club, founded in 1975. Over the years, the organization awarded me the Distinguished Service Award, the Ombudswoman Award, recognized me as the Women's History Honoree, and presented me with the Sojourner Truth Award, the highest honor bestowed on a member by the National Association of NBPW. Gwendolyn and I have become best friends and neighbors.

After no contact with Charles about the children, one day, Edmond, now 16 and Kim, now 14, came home and said, "Frank, we want our last name changed to Moss." They both wrote a letter explaining their decision.

Frank told them to ask me about their idea. After much debate with the children, I said, "I will call our attorney." The attorney drew up the papers for the name change in 1977, and the hearing occurred in 1978. It took about one year. The attorney sent documents to Charles to complete and return when he drew up the papers for the name change. The attorney never heard back from him.

After the children requested to change their last name from Darden to Moss and the courts approved it, Charles, came to our home in Hurst and said no one had informed him. Frank, did not want to be blamed; he had nothing to do with the name change. The children and the attorney completed the process with my permission. I told Charles the attorney sent him the paperwork when the process began months before the court date to the child support address. He could protest or disagree.

Frank told Charles we did not need his money for child support because the children were in high school. What the children needed over the years was for him to show up. They spent many evenings when we lived on Ramey Street in Fort Worth, waiting for him to arrive. Despite this, what they really needed from him was his presence. Unfortunately, he repeatedly failed to show up, leaving them heartbroken and disappointed.

In 1978, Jack and Jill of America, Inc., The Fort Worth Chapter recognized Edmond, and presented him at the 78th Beautillion Ball. The National Association of Negro Business and Professional Women's Club, Inc., sponsored him as a senior at Richland High School. His involvement included the Gyros gymnastics team and the USGF state high school meet in Austin, Texas. What a memorable evening, filled with elegance, tradition, and celebration. His attire included a formal black tuxedo with a white shirt, bow tie and white gloves. I am grateful to organizations like Jack and Jill of America for recognizing our son's achievements and allowing him to shine.

Edmond graduated from Richland Hills High School in 1978 with a four-year academic scholarship to Howard University and the University of Texas in Austin; however, he did not want to attend either school. He took the athletic scholarship in gymnastics from Memphis State University. He left for Memphis State College, although his scholarship did not cover out-of-state tuition. We had to pay the difference in college costs. Frank purchased a new Volvo and gave him his gray Monte Carlo.

The money became tight in our household. With my long-term care knowledge, I created a LTC Nurse consultant business for nursing home facilities. My business provided nursing reviews in nursing homes to locate nursing violations in patient care before the facility's federal and state health inspections. For about a year,

I worked weekends in the emergency room in a hospital on the north side. I did this until Edmond graduated from Memphis State.

He pledged to the Phi Beta Sigma Fraternity, Inc., during his second year in college. Edmond's school was far away, and we missed seeing our son. The distance between Texas and Memphis was about a seven-hour drive. He never met a stranger; he met many new friends in college and a girl named Rorie. They are long-lasting friends today.

Edmond moved into the fraternity house and became vice-president of the chapter and president of the Pan-Hellenic Council. He developed tendonitis in his knees and transferred to the University of Texas at Arlington for a Red Shirt year in 1981. That year, the Grand Prairie YMCA Flyers hired Edmond as a gymnastics coach. Jima Richie coached the Flyers team. The group became a private club named the Spirals Gymnastics Team. He has maintained this relationship as an advising coach for most of his life. He returned to Memphis State University in 1982.

Both my husband and I participated in community events long before entering politics. We received many service awards. While living in Hurst, I was a member of the Women of Rotary of Fort Worth, and Frank was a member of The Rotary Club of Fort Worth. I drove to Ridglea Country Club each month for meetings.

We both now worked in Fort Worth. One day, we talked about moving back home, and Frank located a realtor. Our realtor located a house for sale at 5625 Eisenhower Drive. This was our opportunity to move back to Frank's old neighborhood, Rosedale Park, and become more active and involved in politics. I talked to Kim about commuting back to Richland HS for her senior year.

One of Kim's friends, Lisa Alred, a white girl, invited Kim to her home. During Lisa's senior year, she was the runner-up in the Miss U.S.A. contest. Also, Lisa was on the cheerleader team and helped Kim get on the team. After the other students found out Kim was Lisa's friend, more students started talking to her. In 1980, Kim was the first black student elected to the

Richland H.S. Cheerleader Squad, with the help of her friend, Lisa. Instead of returning to Richland for her senior year, Kim traveled to east Fort Worth during the summer and enrolled in the black school, Dunbar High School, without our knowledge. Frank and I wanted Kim to enroll in Nolan High School. She told us she did not return to Richland because the teachers and students had discriminated against her since the 5th grade. Kim expressed her desire to not attend Nolan due to the low enrollment of black students.

Learning of the racist slurs toward Kim was devastating. She had never told me the students called her nigger in the hallways. Kim shared that the English teacher was incredibly mean to her because she was black. The teacher also gave her low grades and even tried, but failed, to keep her from being a cheerleader. Kim explained that her high school experience was extremely negative. No one invited her to any party during her entire time in Hurst.

Kim faced jealousy and criticism from her classmates while she attended Dunbar. The girls envied her because she spoke standard English. They said she was trying to talk properly. On the other hand, the boys loved her and always tried to date her. Kim's choice of wearing a Neiman Marcus purse and accessories to school made her the target of bullying by the girls. They thought she was a showoff. Even though she had little money, they assumed she had it. Kim wore the samples and items given to her by my niece, Ella, who worked at Neiman's makeup counter. The principal frequently contacted me to come to the school. There was an altercation between Kim and a girl in her class when the girl thought Kim was flirting with her boyfriend. The last time the principal called me to the school, a girl in Kim's class stole her driver's license.

I asked Kim, "Why are you always the center of attention in the principal's office?"

Kim said, "The girls think I am stuck up."

In May 1981, Edmond accompanied her to graduation to prevent the girls from attacking her.

The Fort Worth Assembly, Inc. presented Dr. Mossey Neloice Chadwick Haynes to society in December 1954. I dreamed of having a daughter take part in the assembly ball as well. My dream came true. After graduation, Kim enrolled in Texas Women's University in Denton, Texas. Mattie Gilliam, a friend, and member of the Fort Worth Assembly sponsored her.

In December 1982, the Fort Worth Assembly presented Kimberlen and 14 other young ladies at their 40th annual presentation ball. The Grand Crystal Ballroom of the Hyatt-Regency Hotel hosted the assembly ball. Each debutante took her bow as the band played her favorite song. Kimberlan and 14 other young ladies were presented on a white carpeted stage. They made their promeenages down a white runway from an arch twined with burgundy-hued Vahalla carnations and greenery. Fifteen stunning ladies danced to the live band's music with their fathers and escorts, dressed in traditional white ball gowns. Arrangements of carnations and pom pom mums banked the stage and the runway. Kimberlen's dress was a cream satin 18th-century design with embroidery lace trim, paired with long white kid gloves and a beautiful cascade bouquet of burgundy carnations, cushion mums, and gypsophila with Ming fern. The ladies' escorts wore the traditional black and white tuxedos with a white boutonniere. I am incredibly proud of my sister and Kimberlen for being part of this cherished tradition in our family's history.

Kim lived on campus but did not attend classes often. I removed her from TWU and enrolled her at TCC. She, of course, did not want to attend that school. However, she had to follow my rules if she planned to live at home. It was clear that Kim did not want to attend college. After being dismissed from Saint Joseph Nursing School for reading a book at the nursing station, she entered the armed forces. One Saturday, she stayed out all night, and the next day, she joined the Army. She left that Friday to go to boot camp. She told Frank she had joined the Army. When I found it, I told Frank, "Okay. Maybe the Army will set her on the correct path."

CHAPTER TEN

Life is Full of Surprises

We were empy-nesters. Not too long afterward, I didn't feel well. I thought I had an acute case of gas, or my ulcer was acting up. I went to the doctor, and he ran some tests. The doctor came back in and told me, "Congratulations."

I asked, "For what?"

Then he told me I was pregnant. After 18 years, I could not believe I was pregnant for the third time. My stomach felt nauseated for the entire nine months.

I continued to work and attend all my events. Sigma Chi Epsilon Social Club sponsored my baby shower and it was like no other. The invitations included wives and husbands. The guests gave Franklin Jr. many needed baby gifts; we had items for the next two years.

Mr. and Mrs. Bass, a retired couple who lived next door, also gave us a baby shower. Having more baby gifts for Franklin Jr. elevated my spirits. I was grateful to all the friends who attended my baby showers and provided for our baby's needs, including diaper service. On September 23, 1982, Franklin Douglas Moss Jr. was born at Harris Hospital. Franklin Jr. was born with his nights and days mixed up; he did not sleep at night. It appeared when daylight came, he closed his eyes and slept. We were two exhausted parents. Kim was still at TWU. She had a strategy she used to help Franklin Jr. sleep. When she came home from TWU on the weekend, Franklin Jr. would sleep for her while she listened to hip-hop music.

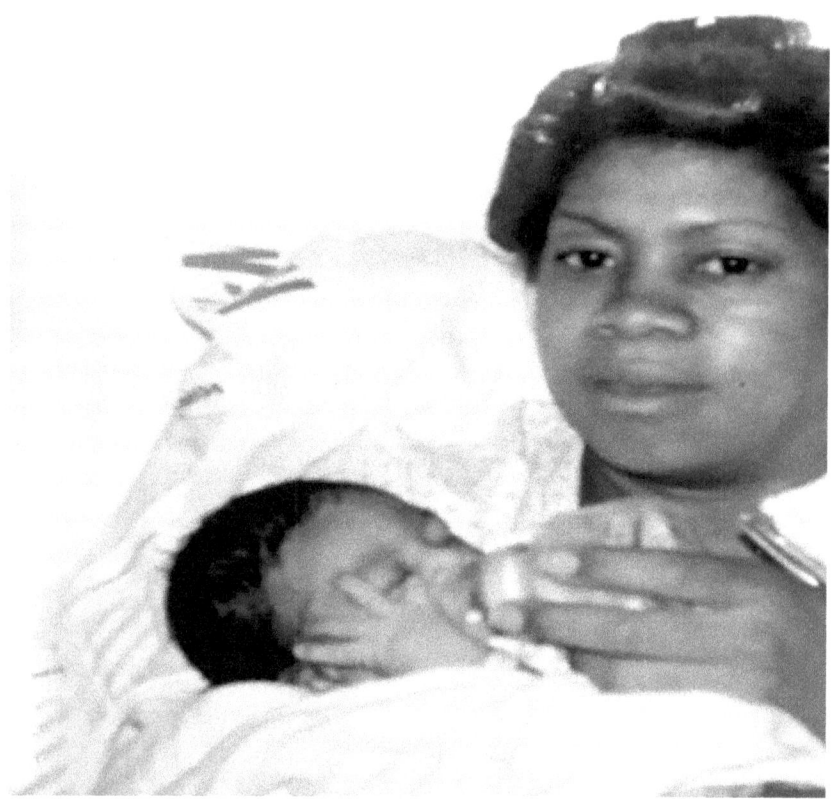

Our little bundle of joy arrived on September 23, 1982.

After I was off work for six weeks, we hired a lady from our church, Jenet Brown, to babysit Franklin Jr. To get more rest, I cut my maternity leave short. Work was less stressful. Sister Brown was God-sent. She told me Franklin Jr. cried so much because he was hungry. She cut a hole in the bottle's nipple and fed Franklin Jr. baby cereal. He stopped crying after he had a full belly.

Going to church was my goal each Sunday. My routine consisted of getting dressed up and driving to church without being responsible for anyone else. One Sunday, the usher who stood in the door of the sanctuary, stopped me as I entered and asked, "Chris, where is the baby?" I was glad Frank did not see me; he had arrived earlier to sing. My car could not get back home fast enough. Franklin Jr. was still sitting in his car seat, looking around the room. Forgive me for leaving my baby home alone. I told myself then, *Girl, you must slow down.*

School was my goal again, and I was ready to go to the next level. Obtaining my master's degree kept rolling over in my mind. With life settling down, I enrolled in Texas Woman's University, Dallas campus. My major was hospital administration. The commute was only 45 minutes twice weekly. Commencement occurred in May 1984. I marched and received my Master of Science degree.

The family was excited when Edmond graduated from Memphis State in 1983 with his Bachelor of Science in Finance, Insurance, and Real Estate. We cheered as he crossed the stage. Franklin Jr., his four-month-old brother, rested across his shoulder as he walked around. Edmond's career began in Mortgage Banking, Relocation Management, Real Estate Management, and Sales. Kim enlisted in the Army in 1983, attended basic training in Charleson, South Carolina, and then transferred to Fort Riley in Kansas. While in Kansas, Kim met George Simpson. She called home several months later and told us she and George were planning their wedding. Kim's wedding day was a culmination of joy and hope. She was always close to her father, Charles, and when she decided to marry George, she eagerly called her father and asked him to give her away. Charles agreed, and the family traveled to Kansas to attend the wedding. Radiant in her wedding gown and flowers, Kim eagerly awaited her father's arrival.

However, when Charles didn't show up, the unexpected absence was a shock. I advised Kim not to wait any longer and proceed with the wedding. Understandably hurt, she received support from Frank who stepped in to give her away. He reminded her that life doesn't always go as planned and assured her he would be there for her if she needed anything. Soon after, her daughter, Kristen Monea, was born. From Kansas, the family transferred to the army base in Pirmasens, Germany.

Zeta Phi Beta Sorority, Inc. Psi Zeta Chapter, my Sorors encouraged me to pledge Zeta: To my left is Alberta Thomas and to my right is Basileus Hazel Wilson.

Hazel Wilson and my neighbor Alberta Thomas encouraged me to pledge to the Zeta Phi Beta Sorority Psi Zeta Chapter. After much dialoguing and reading about the sorority, I committed. The Psi Zeta chapter performed the Archonian Club induction ceremony on March 28, 1981. Soror Hazel Simmons, the Basileus at the time, and Soror Alberta Thomas, Dean of Pledges, welcomed me into the chapter. My Big Sister, Soror Robbie D. Brown, was also there to greet me. I have a deep love for all my blue and white sorors. This is how it went down.

I was frightened because of the rumors I had heard about what I had to perform, including eating worms (the worms turned out to be noodles). The event occurred in Soror Thomas's home. While pledging Zeta Phi beta, the Sorors had me sit on the couch and lay my head back. I heard a soror say, "Open your mouth." I hesitated, then opened my mouth. I felt wet, slimy worms sliding down my throat, which made me feel sick. Afterward, Soror Wilson told me the slimy things were only noodles. My probate letter from Soror Robbie Brown arrived on February 11, 1984. Zeta Phi Beta Sorority, Psi Zeta Chapter, Fort Worth added my name to the roll as Soror Christene Chadwick Moss. I love my blue and white.

I had the pleasure of meeting Soror Sheryl Underwood, a dear friend of mine and a Diamond Life Member of the Zeta Phi Beta sorority. She is a fantastic philanthropist and co-host of "The Talk" show. I was thrilled when she visited Fort Worth twice to attend our unique events.

My Soror Sheryl Underwood, Franklin and me. Underwood, co-host of "The Talk," was a special guest at the 75th anniversary celebration of Zeta Phi Beta Sorority, Inc. Psi Zeta Chapter.

During our 75th anniversary celebration, Sheryl was the special guest of the Zeta Phi Beta Sorority, Inc. Psi Zeta Chapter, and she was also a special guest for the second time for our joint Founders Day in 2013. Soror Underwood's presence kept the guests in tears and laughter all night. It was an unforgettable experience, and Frank and I enjoyed every moment. We even posed proudly with her for a photo to cherish this beautiful memory forever.

It's funny how you look back over your life and see which activities and involvement played a significant role. The most valuable event in my early years was joining an investment group in 1985, "Polytechnic Adventurers." It was a broad experience. Three investors, Shirley Johnson, Mary Lou Watkins, and Lou Brooks told me that the 20 ladies wanted me to join this newly formed group of women. Surprisingly, I was one of two ladies of color in the group.

The Polytechnic community was revitalizing the neighborhood. Our group purchased two storefronts across the street from Texas Wesleyan College. Both structures required extensive renovation before they were usable. While the properties were under construction, the group allowed me to use one space for storing and assembling my campaign signs for my first unsuccessful election campaign in 1986. Once the company renovated the building, both became rental properties. We all came from diverse backgrounds and had various levels of expertise in investing. However, we shared a common goal of wanting to grow our wealth and secure our financial futures. It's been empowering to learn from each other and support one another as we navigate the investing world. I learned much about investing; this was my first financial investment collaboration.

Franklin Jr. was four years old when we received a late-night phone call from a Dallas hospital on October 2, 1985. The caller said, "Edmond Moss, your son, has been in a car accident on Greenville Ave. He is in the hospital in Dallas. You need to come now."

We called Sister Brown and asked if she would watch Franklin Jr. as there had been an accident. We immediately took him to her home around 2:30 a.m. When Frank and I entered the intensive care unit, I could only see a mist surrounding Edmond's bed. I immediately fell to my knees and broke down, crying. Kim had transferred to Germany a month earlier. Frank contacted Kim, and the Army approved an emergency leave. She flew home to see her brother. The doctor explained the details of Edmond's car accident. When we saw his legs, I could only pray. "Lord, ease his pain; have mercy on my son!" The right leg was almost blue, with a gray hue because of a lack of blood and oxygen. The doctor told us he needed surgery immediately on his left leg, and the right leg needed amputation. According to Edmond, he turned when he saw the car and jumped as high as he could. The car caught him in the legs and not in his essential organs. Still, after the doctor amputated Edmond's right leg, he had 27 surgeries on his left leg. His hospital stay included three months of rehabilitation. By the Grace of God, he made it. His healing included sessions with a psychologist, Dr. Brenda Walls. Her time with him significantly affected his recovery. After several months in the hospital, he came home.

In 1987, Edmond later established Elm Realty. In 1990, he married Lisa Renee Nealy and bought a home in Forest Hills. They divorced in 1992. He was hired by JPS in accounts receivable and promoted to Sr. Accountant in accounts payables, however, he left to operate Elm Realty.

He continued his education at Texas Wesleyan University, graduating with his Master of Science in Accounting in May 2003. Then he established Moss Books LLC, a bookkeeping business. Edmond works with many community and civic organizations and has received many awards, trophies, and certificates. Wedding bells rang again in 2005 when he married Jeanine Marie Thomas. They had a daughter, Madeleine Marie Moss, but divorced in 2008. In 2012, the executive director of the Phi Beta Sigma Fraternity Inc., Daryl Anderson, hired him as a staff accountant at headquarters in Washington, D.C. At this writing, he remains at the Phi Beta Sigma headquarters.

While stationed in Germany, Kim and George had their second child, Jorgette, in Kaiserslautern, Germany. Franklin Jr. and I traveled overseas to help Kim with the baby. I can't help but recall the challenge of traveling solo with a five-year-old The 11-hour flight was grueling, and I was exhausted when we arrived. As my mother would say, I was "fit to be tied." Throughout the flight, Franklin Jr. wore out a pair of shoes, as he walked up and down the aisles, and chatted with anyone who would listen. The other passengers enjoyed his company despite his noisiness. By the time we landed in Germany, he knew the names of everyone on the flight.

I enjoyed the beautiful architecture of the buildings and the snow every morning while visiting Germany. Franklin Jr. got up early every morning to watch the snow and become excited while watching it melt in the afternoon. After that tour of duty, George and Kim transferred to Fort Hood in Killeen, Texas. In 1990, Kim's tour of duty ended with an honorable discharge.

One day, I heard the telephone ring. It was Kim. The Vocational Nursing Central Texas College in Austin, Texas, had approved her application to enroll in nursing school. Her acceptance letter followed. The nursing school's graduation occurred in June 1994. The state exam was a breeze for Kim. While sitting with Kim after graduation, she reminded me of the car accident we were involved in while living in Hurst, Texas.

The accident happened in 1975, when I worked at a nursing home. There was ice on the ground, and snow was falling. Frank told me not to go to work because the weather was getting worse. How could I forget this incident? I told Frank that the vehicle could make it through the snow. We packed our clothes and headed to work. Kim was in the car with me. We were only in the car for a short while. Our street ended at the stop sign, where I had to turn left or right. When I arrived at the stop sign, I stepped lightly on the brakes. My car continued moving through the stop sign to the other side of the road and into the ditch. The vehicle lost the front fender. That accident frightened me. Frank never had to tell me again to stay home when ice or snow was on the ground. After that, I learned to curl up on the couch and make myself at home.

I was considering a career change when I received a call from John Peter Smith Hospital. They informed me they were building a health clinic in my neighborhood, Stop Six. People in the community had requested that the hospital hire me to operate the Stop Six Health Center. They had observed me providing care to individuals and felt I was the right person for the job. This news thrilled me, and I eagerly awaited the opportunity. The hospital hired and trained me at other outreach clinics in 1992. The Stop Six Health Center officially opened in 1994 and had a complete staff, medical equipment, and furniture. The hospital named me the director of the center.

I worked as the health center supervisor, which allowed me to serve a community in need of healthcare services and provide job opportunities for those interested in healthcare within the

Front Row (left to right): Wanda Gipson, Director Community Outreach Services; Christene Moss, Health Center Supervisor; Harriet Hilliard, M.D., Medical Director; Drenda Witt, Director Public Relations; Back Row (left to right): Larry Wallace, Associate Administrator; Lee Roy McCurley, M.D., Staff Physician

community. The JPS medical interns kept us extremely busy, and the biggest challenge was ensuring we had enough appointments available to meet our client's needs. We had many clients who required our services. I collaborated with the nursing staff, such as Marva, Essie, Dian, Janell, Vera, and many others, including the medical interns and physicians. We implemented goals to provide medical and specialty care such as obstetrics, prenatal care, infectious disease treatment, and internal medicine. The clinic also offered laboratory and radiology services and wellness education classes for our clients. I enjoyed the culture and working conditions at the health clinic; although, at the end of the day, the staff and I would be exhausted and ready to leave duty.

The Vocational Nurses Licenses exam was easy for Kim. In 1996, she and George shipped out from Killeen to Fort Bragg in Fayetteville, North Carolina, near his parents. In 2000, I called George and asked, "George, where is my family? You left here four years ago with my daughter going to Fayetteville and I have not seen her since." I told him to bring her home. The following Christmas, George drove the family home to Texas and spent time with our family. Later, he retired. He had told her they would move to a place between the two families once he retired. However, George had no intention of moving. Divorce was on the horizon in Fayetteville. In 2008, Kim returned to Texas after her divorce.

We had enrolled Franklin Jr. into daycare at six months old. The family had many days and nights adjusting to a new baby, especially me, after 18 years. At one year old, it was time for the first haircut. Thank God. His hair was so long and thick that it took me forever to style it. What a show; the barber's chair shook while he cut his hair. I did not know if I should feel sorry for Mr. Moss, the barber, his grandfather, or myself. I could barely hold Franklin Jr. between my legs. Mr. Moss cut the best he could with the child's constant movement and crying. After about an hour, we survived that task.

At four years old and two days later, we enrolled Franklin Jr. into pre-kindergarten at White Lake Hills private school. While Franklin Jr. attended school, a little white boy bullied him daily by kicking him in the butt. The teacher and the principal talked with the boy and the boy's parents. The boy continued to kick him. Franklin Sr. and I went to the boy's home and talked with the parents, and the boy stopped kicking him. This little boy was a bully, so disrespectful that he did not obey his parents or any adult at school. The little boy went skiing in Colorado with his parents when school was out for winter break. His parents said they told their son not to play on the snow hill and to return to the group. The little boy went to the pile of snow, anyway. An avalanche occurred and covered the little boy, causing his death. The school provided a child psychologist to ensure Franklin Jr. had no emotional issues resulting from the child's death.

In first grade, Franklin Jr. enrolled in piano classes. His first-grade teacher wanted to retain him because she said he was too small and would never be a leader. The teacher kept him in the class with another student who was not performing well. We moved him to Mrs. Dixon's private school on the south side of Fort Worth. There, he learned how to read and write in second grade. All the up-and-rising black children in Fort Worth attended Mrs. Dixon's school. She taught gifted and non-gifted students. I enrolled him in second-grade public school because of the pressure from the community and political reasons after my school board election.

Franklin Jr.'s mouth always got him in trouble; he was curious about everything. He questioned the teacher's statements and actions. He often raised his hand and asked the teacher "Why?" different activities occurred. At church one Sunday, the minister stated, "God created the world and everything in it!"

He asked our minister, "You said God made the whole world, then who made God?" Rev. had no answer; he only shook his head.

Franklin Jr. graduated from David K. Sellars Elementary School and transferred to the Dunbar Middle School magnet program. However, he continued to be curious about the subject matter of his studies and excelled in most classes. Most programs at the school included Frank and me. Volunteering was popular during the time he attended school. He had excellent teachers at Dunbar Middle School. Dunbar High School was the next school of choice for him. I could not persuade him to attend Southwest, Arlington Heights, or Paschal High School. He preferred to enroll in our neighborhood school with his friends. My thoughts traveled back to the discrimination Kim experienced in a predominately white school during high school. So, Frank and I agreed with his choice.

At Dunbar, he met many young men and their parents. The Distinguished Gentlemen, an organization in Dunbar for boys, taught young men life skills. The events Franklin and his friends attended created a bond and a lifelong friendship. My home was an open door for all his friends. Young men were always hungry; I would bring leftover food from the banquets and leave it in the refrigerator. Franklin and his friends would come over at lunch and eat. My home became a safe house and the place they came to chill. Even after leaving for college and returning home, they remain best friends and plan group activities.

In September 1998, Franklin Jr., had a negative experience with the police while in high school. He and his friends were in the car traveling home through the Polytechnic community. The police stopped them. My son was so distraught when he arrived home because of how the police had treated them. He was in tears and told us the police had stopped them, made them get out of the car, and lie on the ground as they talked to them like they had stolen something. He said he told the police repeatedly who he was, who his parents were, and that he and his friends were riding home and had not done anything.

Franklin Jr. had learned about "Driving While Black" and discrimination from his father. It shocked him when it happened; he realized the police had stopped his car because they saw a group of black boys riding through the neighborhood. We spent the night calming Franklin Jr. down enough for him to go to sleep.

Both of us are members of Jack and Jill of America, Inc. Fort Worth Chapter. The organization presented Franklin Jr. in the 2000 Beautillion, a prestigious group of young men who have taken their passage into adulthood.

During his high school years, Franklin Jr. actively took part in various organizations and events. One of his notable achievements was serving as the treasurer of the youth group of Jack and Jill of America, Inc. Fort Worth Chapter. The group was involved in various activities across the city and the state. Additionally, he was engaged in Natural Helpers, Honors Choir, Elite P.N.B. Steppers, Worldwide Prospects, Distinguished Gentlemen of Dunbar, JROTC, NAACP Youth, Our City, Our Children with the city of Fort Worth, Community Builders Youth Volunteer, Phi Delta Kappa, and Fannie Mae Heath Cultural Club. These organizations recognized his volunteerism and leadership abilities.

When he graduated from Dunbar, it was an exciting time for me, as I was the school board member who presented him with his high school diploma. It brought me joy to give my son his certificate. Prairie View A.M. University accepted him after he graduated from Dunbar High School in 2000. Franklin Jr. left for college as my career took another turn.

Although I enjoyed working as the Health Center supervisor at JPS, I retired in 2000 to work for the state in the Texas Department of Aging and Disability Services Department. I found my job at the State Department appealing. As part of my role, I conducted inspections of long-term care facilities and other health care providing agencies. I completed survey reports highlighting deficiencies in nursing facilities, specifically nursing homes. And I recommended remedies and prepared a report to support regulatory regulations based on my findings. Responsibilities included revisiting long-term care facilities to ensure they had corrected any previously cited regulatory violations of both State and Federal standards. Communicating with the residents and being able to solve issues that affected their quality of life was a gratifying aspect of my job.

My career path has been a significant journey, starting from a long-term care facility and culminating at the State Department. This progression, from being directly involved in the care of residents to upholding state and federal guidelines for their care, is a testament to my dedication and passion for this field.

During Franklin Jr.'s senior year in high school, we purchased a red Ford Focus for him. However, because of the car's bright color, it often attracted the attention of the police. To avoid any issues, I advised him to wait until his second year of college before taking the car and to use other means of transportation during his first year. He agreed to this plan.

Despite this, only a few weeks into his first year, he called us multiple times and begged his dad to bring the car to him. He expressed his dissatisfaction with his dirty clothes, his mail still being in the office mailbox, and the absence of food in the dining hall by the time he arrived. He also claimed he missed classes because of the long distance he had to walk across the campus. In response, his dad promised to drive the car down that weekend. I spoke to Franklin Jr. and asked, "When did students stop walking across campus to get what they needed or attend classes? Did all the students have cars?" I reminded him that not all students had cars and that he should take advantage of other options available. He had manipulated his dad into getting what he wanted.

While he was away in college, Frank and I were officially empty nesters. When we traveled to Italy with the Sister Cities International group. Frank traveled with the Fort Worth City Council District 5 in partnership with Sister Cities International.

I enjoyed traveling to Italy with the Fort Worth Sister Cities International Ambassador Delegation, representing the City of Fort Worth. Our trip, "A Taste of Italy," took place from August 31 to September 7, 2001, and was a culinary wine tour. We arrived at Milan Malpensa Airport in Frankfurt and met the tour bus that took us to the Grand Hotel Astoria in Reggio Emilia.

On the first day, we explored Reggio Emilia. We visited several interesting sites, including Teatro Valli, the Hall of Tricolore, Basilica Della Ghiara, and the city orientation. We also had a fantastic lunch at Prater restaurant and saw Reggiane Hills, Matilde's Castle and Fortress. The buildings were beautiful and had a medieval and Gothic style that reminded me of the architecture of the 1800s and 1900s. We also visited the Church of Madonna Della Battaglia, Rossena, Canossa Castle, and the ruins.

We visited the Parmigiano Reggiano factory the following day and enjoyed a wine and food tour. That allowed us to see how dairy workers make cheese. We then visited Casali Viticultori of Scandiano, a winegrowing and producing factory, and the Balsamic Vinegar factory. The tour included wine and cheese tasting, and the group purchased wine.

The next day, we attended an exchange planning meeting with the Chamber of Commerce and a lunch meeting with the City Council. We went on other tours, including Parma, Verdi's places, Busseto, and Verona. Lastly, we attended Verdi's Aries' exclusive concert. It was an incredible week full of enjoyment for me and work for Frank.

Thank God, our group landed back home three days before 9/11. The terrorist attacks on September 11, 2001, resulted in the tragic loss of 2,977 lives and left thousands more injured at locations including the World Trade Center, the Pentagon, and in Somerset County, Pennsylvania. Each year, memorial events take place at these three sites to honor and remember those affected by the tragedy.

Frank and me listening to a story of "best wines" at the wine factory in Italy.

Frank and me at the cheese factory observing how they make cheese in an Italy cheese factory.

Hanging out with my daughter, Kimberlen, at the grandkids' birthday party.

My sons, Franklin Jr. and Edmond.

On Grandparents Day at school, I took my grandson, Micah, his favorite Whataburger meal.

Enjoying a cinnamon latte with Franklin Jr. at Black Coffee Fort Worth.

Over the years, I chose the events we attended with my friends. My friend, Windell Lou, invited us to her annual Super Bowl party; I enjoyed this function. Windell Lou put me in the pot in Lake Como. For several years, I won the jackpot. I stopped dragging Frank along because he did not enjoy partying. When he did go with me, before we left home, he always asked, "How long are we going to stay?" That was my cue; he did not want to attend.

When others described Frank as someone who prioritized business, it didn't surprise me. He had more of a business personality. My friends, though, saw that as him not being interested in their gatherings. Frank did not take enough time to enjoy the little stuff. He preferred attending school board or city council events more than engaging in events with friends. He did not believe in celebrating special days, such as wedding anniversaries and birthdays, but he celebrated the Fourth of July and Christmas.

Our marriage had its difficulties, just like other couples. However, we have a good marriage. Several years ago, I said to Frank, "Let's go celebrate our wedding anniversary."

I caught him off guard. He had a gift card to the Cheesecake Factory, therefore, we went. However, he said he could only stay an hour because he had to work. One of his former employees gave him a gift card each year for the two of us to celebrate our wedding anniversary. He did not use the cards for that purpose. We do enjoy other times. For example, we still attend the balls hosted by the Ambassadors and the Fort Worth Assembly each year during the Christmas holiday season. In 2021, we didn't because of the COVID-19 pandemic.

I thank God Frank and I had no problems with our children concerning drugs, alcohol, or unruly behavior in school. My social life was exciting and busy and my calendar stayed full. I attended events with friends, city council, and school board events. Frank and I entertain friends and family at our home during the Christmas holidays. I found joy in building and maintaining

In Washington, D.C., I attended Edmond's place of worship, Shiloh Baptist Church, with him.

friendships and relationships. I still get invites, but as the two of us have become more seasoned, I am more selective about the events I attend nowadays.

The Chadwick family always gather to celebrate the holidays and birthdays. Potluck family dinners are trendy, and I can rely on my brother, Alvin, to cook plenty of food. Donald L and I continue our annual Chadwick Christmas Dinner, the Sunday before Christmas. The dinner is always a hit, with all family members taking part. Those who have passed on are remembered and honored. Their spouses and children step in to take their place.

Daughter-in-law, Mia Moss sitting on the fireplace holding left to right, Ayri, and Franklin III. Sitting far right is granddaughter, Kristen Simpson Vance, holding Ahri. On the floor is Madeleine, Micah, and Jorgette.

Everyone knew Alvin for his delicious pans of ribs, green beans, and potato salad. The people from the Dallas area always leave us impressed with their cooking. My niece, Michaella Titus, prepares soups, cobblers, cabbage, and salads for the entire family. Harold, my nephew, takes over for his mother and family, bringing stacks of pies, sweet potato, apples, and chess pies. My great niece, Yolanda, is always ready to whip up any dessert or dish. Another niece, Carolyn, takes over for Virginia and brings all the drinks

My family enjoys our annual Christmas Day tradition. Frank, me, Franklin Jr., Mia, Kimberlen and Edmond.

and condiments for dinner. After Alvin passed away, Stacy and Deborah took over most of the planning, and stepped in for Howard. Winstona (Laythette), my sister-in-law, took over for Adolphus, and brings her finger-licking greens. In contrast, my sister-in-law, Joyce stands in for Bruce and makes a delicious broccoli casserole. Elder E.T. and my sister-in-law, Bertha, bring our favorite red beans and hot water cornbread. Donald L and Allean, my sister-in-law, cook up big pans of chicken and dressing, and they also make a five-layer German chocolate cake. We all enjoy the delicious food and the company of our loved ones.

CHAPTER ELEVEN

My Life in Politics

I have worked with schools for many years. I loved helping students learn how to read. Before I thought about campaigning for the school board, I was interested in ensuring children learned to read before entering first grade. Mama taught her children that knowledge is power and that learning to read was the basis for success. Parents of color expressed outrage because their children were not learning to read at grade level. I remember how much fun I had reading books, although the books were old and worn during elementary school.

My community encouraged me to enter the FWISD school board election held in 1986; I lost the election to the incumbent, Mrs. Maudrie M. Walton. Mrs. Walton was an institution in the community, with a school named in her honor, M.M. Walton Elementary.

After the election, Mrs. Walton said, "Little girl, you've got guts. I will support you for the next election." And she did. Mrs. Walton retired from the school board in May 1990. I filed to run for the school board seat against four male candidates.

The support from my pastor, Reverend B.W. Lockett, opened the door for me to meet and receive support from other clergy in Fort Worth. He spoke about my character, dedication to helping children, involvement in church activities with children, and why I would be the better trustee. I distributed flyers throughout the community and encouraged people to vote for me.

Mrs. Margaret Jennings called me and said, "Mrs. Moss, I want to help with your campaign." She heard my speeches, and my voice convinced her I was sincere and wanted to help children succeed. With a map in hand, she walked me all over District 3, knocking on doors and greeting people. She told me, "You do not have to have money to go and ask people to vote for you." Forest Hill was in District 3, and I called my niece in Dallas for help. Ella Davis, her brother, Harold Davis, and others came to my rescue on election day; they walked Forest Hill and got out the vote.

I learned that Mrs. Mary Grigsby, my high school teacher, lived in Forest Hill. Mrs. Grigsby told Ella, "Tell Christene to run like she never ran before." Then she gave Ella a donation for me. She told Ella to let me know she was supporting my campaign. My hard work during the 1990 school board election to represent District 3 was a success.

The Greater Fort Worth Area Negro Business and Professional Women's Club, Inc. 1990. Members front row: Alice Powell, Betty Franklin, Eloise Spivey, me, and Delores Simmons. Back row left to right: Verneda Sanders, Betty Senegal, Beverly Washington, Hazel Simmons, and Cora Miller. Gwendolyn Morrison is not pictured. (Personal collection of Beverly Washington)

I conducted my writing and telephone campaign from the voter's list in my dining room. I had help from my organization, The Greater Fort Worth Area Negro Business and Professional Women Inc., the late Hazel Wilson and Alberta Thomas, Dr. Gwendolyn Morrison, Deloise Simmons, Beverly Washington, Veneda Sanders, and Alice Powell. Others included James Etta Brooks, Sharon Moss, and Greta Moss. They purchased and mailed all the campaign materials for my campaign.

My church sisters, the matrons, Jessie Curry, Clayetta Curry, Marva Lewis, Opal Harris, and others, helped place labels on my campaign literature. I left boxes of literature with labels at their homes. After they labeled all the materials, I drove by, picked up my campaign literature, and headed to the post office.

The midnight riders, my girlfriends since third grade, the late Charlene McLane Adams, Windell Lou Hall Elzy, and Barbara Curly Mitchell rode and placed campaign signs in yards during the night. I would call and ask, "Are the four musketeers ready to ride?" We had fun reminiscing as we rode. I won the 1990 school board election to represent District 3.

The Fort Worth ISD school board president, Gary Manny, read the oath of office. After repeating the oath, I took my seat as the District 3 representative alongside the other school board trustees.

On May 9, 1990, Gary Manny read my sworn-in papers to the Fort Worth ISD school board as a trustee. "Christene Moss, raise your right hand." When Mrs. Walton relinquished her board seat to me, I was nervous. My feet clapped while I sat at that dais. I looked up at all those white people and said, "God, only one black person is sitting up there. What have I gotten myself into? What am I going to do?"

When the school board meeting ended, I unglued myself from the seat. I wondered if the board noticed I was as scared as a jackrabbit. I had to hold my fingers to keep my hand still from moving and shaking.

I called Ms. Walton, the former board member and said, "I must talk to you about the school board."

She laughed aloud and said, "Okay, little girl. Come on over. Come on over." Her home was one and a half blocks from mine. I was always open to her sharing nuggets of knowledge. Boy, I ate our meeting up.

I constantly called her for advice, and she always responded, "Come on over, let's talk." She was my inspiration. Mrs. Walton was a kind, humble, and seasoned neighbor. She had experience and knowledge and wanted to share it with me. She was an exemplary principal, and the school had an A rating during her tenure.

My hard work during the 1990 school board election to represent District 3 was a success. FWISD initiated a program to improve students' reading on grade level in all schools, especially students on the east side of town.

Campaigning for re-election to the Fort Worth School Board as school board trustee representing District 3, rolled around every four years. Cold chills ran up and down my spine. I couldn't afford to rent space for a campaign office; therefore, my election campaigns took place in our den, using multiple folding tables. My telephone bank team worked from my home and, after a few years, worked from their own locations. The re-election campaign stressed all households for at least four months before election day.

Being nervous during your campaign is okay. You always want to take the voters seriously. Why? Because you are continuously determining if constituents will vote for you as their first choice of candidate.

Franklin Jr. was my sidekick, and he loved going on the campaign trail. His favorite task was delivering campaign signs with my photo on them. He also loved fast food and knew we would stop at McDonald's at the end of the day. Yet, we always carved out a block of time for family time. Campaign rallies energized my family and the campaign workers. One year, we used my vacant rental house for the re-election campaign. Franklin Jr. was old enough to work in the telephone bank, calling constituents.

Franklin Jr. asked, "Mother, why do you work so hard during re-election?"

My answer was always the same. "Remember, the people can vote you into an office, and the people can vote you out of office."

The next four years rolled around, and he and his friends formed a walking group. This group walked door to door, encouraging constituents in District 3 to vote for me. His friends always had campaign flyers to distribute wherever they traveled.

Donald L., supported my campaign by decorating his truck with a billboard of me and my messages, "Vote for Christene Chadwick Moss" and "It's All About the Children." He drove around District 3, and encouraged people to vote for me. We won the election and made a real difference in our constituents' lives.

During my campaign, my school board account had a low balance. Fortunately, my campaign manager and his wife, Attorney Jesse Gaines and Gwenda Burns, provided in-kind donations and office space for our telephone bank, which was crucial to our success. Attorney Gaines continued to be my campaign manager for every re-election until my retirement, and he also managed Frank's re-election campaign for Fort Worth City Council.

One morning, the school district called and told me that retired General Colin Powell had invited a team of educators to

Philadelphia, Pennsylvania, to attend the President's Summit for America's Future. "Do you want to attend and represent FWISD," I was asked.

I immediately said, "Yes, I will go!"

On April 27-29, 1997, I joined ten other Fort Worth delegates chosen to attend. Our group traveled by private plane.

Standing left to right, I stood far left with Mayor Kenneth Barr standing tall next to Dr. Jennifer Brooks. Also sitting in the middle, former President and First Lady Bush, and Bob Ray Sanders.

Retired General Colin Powell organized the event. The summit aimed to gather educators from across the country to develop a plan to provide five fundamental resources to an additional 2 million young people by the end of 2000.

In addition to General Powell, notable speakers included President William J. Clinton, Oprah Winfrey, Jesse Jackson, Barbara Bush, Nancy Reagan, Vice President Albert Gore and other prominent figures. The task assigned to each delegation was to develop a preliminary plan to achieve the shared national goal in their respective communities or states. Our group met with President Clinton and General Colin Powell, who spoke about the summit's goal.

Upon returning to Fort Worth, our delegation planned a community meeting and drafted a strategy to reach our goal.

Christene Moss in Philadelphia, part of the delegates representing Fort Worth Attending the "**Presidents' Summit for America's Future**" Chaired by General Colin Powell. Talked with President Clinton and former president George Bush.

President Clinton stands to the left of me. Next to me is Major Barr and far right is Father Hasso.

Excitement filled the room at Forest Oak Middle School when, in early 1996, Governor George W. Bush traveled to FWISD, talked with the students, and emphasized the importance of reading. I thanked the governor for visiting a southeast FWISD school. The students were engaged and looked on with excitement as he spoke. He told them, "You must read every day, even if you do not want to." Assistant Superintendent Morris Holmes and school board members accompanied him to the school. While visiting Wyatt High School, Governor Bush emphasized to administrators, "It is important not to allow social promotion in high school!" (*Fort Worth Star-Telegram Newspaper*)

Governor Bush posed for a photo with me when he visited Forest Oak Middle School in Fort Worth ISD in early 1996. HE encouraged students to read. (*Fort Worth Star-Telegram Newspaper*)

Once I won the election in 1990, Frank became obsessed with being an elected official. He studied how to become elected to the Fort Worth City Council. At some point, it became a competitive situation in our marriage.

Frank approached me one day and said, "I am going to be on the City Council one day." He said it many more times.

My answer was always the same: "Sure you will."

He became aggressive with the idea of becoming an elected official at all costs. He served as the representative of District 5 on the Fort Worth City Council from August 1998 through May 2004.

He stepped down from the Fort Worth City Council and made an unsuccessful bid for the Tarrant County Commissioners seat. The community re-elected him to the Fort Worth City Council to represent District 5 from May 2007-May 2013. During Frank's tenure on the City Council, he was an effective councilman and made many significant decisions for District 5.

In 2002, I spurred the development of the innovative "Academic English for Success" (A.E.S.) program. The program fosters mastery of Standard English and its use by developing strong verbal and written communication skills for appropriate contexts. During school visits, I observed that many English-speaking students needed to speak or write Standard English. I reminded my fellow trustees and staff that students unable to communicate appropriately would face lifelong negative consequences. I challenged the team to design a program promoting Standard English at school while respecting the vernacular children used at home or with friends. The A.E.S. program was a success. In 2006, there was a change in FWISD superintendents; the program was dissolved without notice to educators or principals.

I watched Senator Barack Obama's television advertisement in his campaign for the President of the United States. The advertisements ignited my hope in the vote. He looked young and fresh, had an olive skin tone, and he was handsome. His intelligence impressed me, and I knew he would make a great president. I was even more convinced I wanted to campaign for him when I saw him in person. Black elected officials in Tarrant County received a message to attend Senator Barack Obama's campaign rally in Fort Worth, Texas, on February 28, 2008, at the Fort Worth Convention Center. Eleven thousand people filled the convention center. The elected officials were backstage and took individual photos with Senator Obama. Hearing his voice and speech motivated the group to work on his campaign. His "Yes We Can" message resonated with everyone at the rally. The chant became infectious, and everyone sang as they left the gathering.

In 2008, Senator Barack Obama became the 44th President of the United States. We did it!

Frank and I received an invitation to the White House from Congressman Marc Veasey to the Inaugural celebrations in Washington D. C. There were jubilant celebrations across the country. We attended the event at the Historic YWCA's elegant ballroom. Frank gave the occasion for that night's event. (*The Black Voice Fort Worth- Arlington Edition*, Thursday, January 22– Wednesday, January 28, 2009.)

I met President Barack Obama while campaigning in Fort Worth, Texas, in 2008.

When Frank took office on the City Council to serve District 5, Franklin Jr. was in the 10th grade. We travelled to many cities on business responsibilities related to each elected board. As two elected officials who were husband and wife, we became known as "The Power Couple. I earned the status of Master School Board Trustee of the Leadership Texas Association of School Boards

(TASB). One morning in 2001, I received a call from my Como High School teacher and mentor, Ms. Grigsby. She told me she had been following my career and saw that I was the only school board member who listened to parents, students, the community, and school staff over the years. I listened to the parents' voices when I won the school board election. I was the first board member to conduct forums to receive input from the community and then follow through to ensure parents received answers to their questions. She further stated that the communities I represented, Stop-Six and the Polytechnic neighborhoods, recommended that the name Eastland Elementary School be renamed Christene Chadwick Moss Elementary School. I responded, "Thank you, Mrs. Grisgby, for this special honor. I will continue to support and listen to our schools, parents, students, and community."

I am sitting with Mrs. Gale Lewis, the first principal of Christene Chadwick Moss Elementary. After Eastland Elementary was renamed, Mrs. Lewis took the reins, and we created a new school culture.

On June 13, 2001, FWISD changed the name of Eastland Elementary to Christene Chadwick Moss Elementary) in my honor. The Salvation Army named its children's library in my honor for helping to establish a facility for homeless students.

The school named in my honor: Christene Chadwick Moss Elementary.

Volunteering at my namesake Christene C. Moss Elementary School. Principal Charla Wright Staten, second person from the right, and staff receiving school donations for students.

For 125 years in FWISD, no black school board member held the president's title or seat. In 2010, I led an effort to involve the Justice Department in transforming the FWISD Board of Education into nine single-member districts. In 2013, I became the first African American board president and the first African American woman board president. In 2002, I was board president for a short while when the sitting president died.

I held the following offices during my time of service:

- Vice President / 1996-1998
- Vice President / 2000-2002
- President / March 2002 – May 2002 (Due to the untimely death of the sitting president)
- Vice President / 2008-2013
- Secretary / January 2013 – July 2013
- President / 2013-2014
- 1st Vice President / 2014-2016
- 2nd Vice President / 2017-2018

During my nearly three decades on the FWISD Board, I focused on students' educational welfare and supportive resources for their families. Under my leadership, the FWISD explored and then implemented the concept of single-gender academies. I traveled to New York City, Austin, Texas, and other cities to examine single-gender schools' efficacy in a public school district. Under my leadership, the district established the Young Women's Leadership Academy (YWLA) and the Paul Laurence Dunbar Young Men's Leadership Academy (YMLA), Gold Seal Schools of Choice. The two schools continue to receive accolades and national recognition for the achievements of their students.

Our team completely renovated YMLA with brand-new classrooms and a first-class competition gymnasium. I helped to establish the Gold Seal Aviation Engineering Program at Dunbar. Further, I supported the construction of the state-of-the-art aviation hangar on the Dunbar campus. Renovations also included a new field house.

With both of us in the spotlight as elected officials, family time and quality time for our son was paramount. Along the journey, we aimed to expose him to as many community, state, and national leaders as possible when we traveled. We didn't use a babysitter when we attended most events; he traveled with us.

We enjoyed what we did for the community. We were both heavily involved in community activities before we became elected officials. I have received over 100 plaques, trophies, and awards for community service work.

We enjoyed traveling together and attending events over the years. One day, we realized we were not spending any time at home. Finally, we had to stop and take care of our home life.

Franklin Jr. knew all the school board members well. One of the board trustees, Jean McClung, and her husband, John, attended most of the school board conferences. John took Franklin Jr. on every tour around the various cities. He enjoyed visiting cities like New York, Miami, San Diego, San Francisco, Las Vegas, Florida, Washington D.C., and other places, especially the ones with youth activities.

When he was nine, he visited the White House, which was quite impressive. Our Congressman, Martin Frost, facilitated it for constituents to see. Houston, Texas, had been one of his favorite places since his uncle Frank lived there. Frank kept a guest room for visiting siblings if we stayed overnight.

My brother would collect us from the hotel and take us out to eat. After a while, when Franklin Jr. had traveled enough, he told me, "Mother, please, no more traveling for me."

An unveiling of the Christene Chadwick Moss portrait occurred on January 14, 2015. I received a call from Principal Charla Staten. She asked, "Mrs. Moss, come by the school. It will only take a minute." I explained I did not have a babysitter. She reiterated, "It is okay. We will not take long."

Franklin and I enjoying a birthday party as empty nesters.

The unveiling of the Christene Chadwick Moss Portrait took place in 2015. On the left are Franklin Sr. and me. On the right is Dr. Gwendolyn Morrison.

Once I entered the building, I saw the staff had placed blue and white balloons everywhere. Photos from my career hung up and down the hallways. It was a surprise reception and recognition sponsored by the principals and teachers of District 3 and the community for 25 years of school board service.

Unveiling of the Christene Chadwick Moss Portrait: Sajade Miller gave me a plaque of appreciation. Across the front row: Dr. Carlos Walker, Mr. Rod White, me, SaJade Miller, Rochelle Horton, Dr. Cherie Washington, Latres Cole, Ricky Brown, and Seretha Lofton.

All of the accolades from elected officials were overwhelming. Reverend Jack A. Crane, the minister of True Vine Baptist Church, located across the street from the school gave kind words of appreciation. He thanked me for my service as a school board member. In 2003, Reverend Crane and his congregation adopted the Christene C. Moss Elementary School. All three principals of that school were present. Mrs. Gail Lewis was the principal when the name change occurred; they promoted her downtown to the administration building.

The second principal was Mrs. Seretha Lofton, who moved to the middle school as principal. The current principal at Christene C. Moss is Mrs. Charla Staten. I brought my grandson, Franklin

Moss III, to the event in a car seat. I didn't have time to find a babysitter. The attendees were gracious in assisting me with him. Elected officials, ministers, the community, school staff, and students presented many resolutions, proclamations, certificates, student presentations, paintings, songs, and gifts. School staff, administrators, community friends, and politicians came from Fort Worth ISD. I could not hold back the tears of joy, and spent most of my time saying, "Thank you."

Congressman Marc Veasey recorded a video from the floor of the House of Representatives, "Mr. Veasey, Mr. Speaker, and I rise today to honor Christene Chadwick Moss for her twenty-five years of service to the students and schools of Fort Worth as a member of the Fort Worth ISD Board of Education." Veasey further stated, "In honor of Mrs. Moss's twenty-five years of dedicated service to the Fort Worth community and its schools, the Senate will enter this statement into the congressional record on Wednesday, January 13, 2016."

Congressman Veasey's office presented me with a written copy of the Congressional Record, Proceedings, and Debates of the 114th Congress First Session. Commissioner Roy Charles Brooks, Precinct No. 1, bestowed me with a Resolution from Tarrant County, Texas. Mayor Betsy Price and the Fort Worth City Council presented me with a Proclamation from the City of Fort Worth.

State Senator Konni Burton, District 10, introduced me with The State of Texas Resolution. State Representative Nicole Collier, District 95, gave me The State of Texas Resolution and State Representative Charlie Geren, District 99, accorded me with The State of Texas House of Representative Certificate of Merit plaque.

The honors continued with City Council Representative for District 5, Gyna Bivens, presented me with a plaque of recognition for community service. Texas Senator Royce West, District 23, Dallas, gave me The Texas State Senate Certificate of Recognition for 25 years of school board service for the Fort Worth Independent School District.

Congressman Marc Veasey, supporting my years of service on the FWISD School Board as a Trustee.

Under my leadership, the district has also passed four groundbreaking school bond proposals in 2007, 2011, 2013, and 2017. With the assistance of the Dunbar Alumni, I helped rename Dunbar Middle School in honor of the late James Martin Jacquet. He served 37 years as an educator in the FWISD, first as a mathematics teacher and then as principal. Even though I am retired from the FWISD Board of Education, I represented the district as a director of the Texas Association of School Boards (TASB) and Master School Board Trustee of Leadership TASB. My work is long and distinguished. I served on the FWISD Equity Committee and the FWISD 2017 Bond Oversight Committee.

I have been a life member of the Fort Worth Chapter of the National Association for the Advancement of Colored People (NAACP) since 1980. I look forward to the George D. Flemings Memorial Freedom Fund Banquet held every fourth Friday of October. Friday, October 27, 2017, was extraordinary for me. United States Congresswoman Maxine Waters from California was our keynote speaker. Her message permeated the Will Rogers Memorial

Center Round Up Inn with "Freedom for All." Micah and Franklin III, my grandsons, attended and were on the edge of their chairs listening to her every word.

Visiting Senator Royce West of Dallas, District 23 at the Capitol in Austin, Texas to share information about the Texas Caucus of black School Board Members. Senator West has been a friend since the 70s at UTA Arlington.

My daughter-in-law, Mia Owens Moss, holds Franklin III as Congresswoman Maxine Waters hugs my grandson Micah during the NAACP banquet.

For twenty years, I had the pleasure of traveling with my friend, Linda Griffin, the President of the Garland ISD School Board. Our aim was to discover best practices that could enhance student outcomes in our respective school districts, FWISD and Garland ISD. Linda and I worked on various local, state, and national school organizations during this time.

My family at my retirement from the Fort Worth ISD School Board; seated left to right: Bertha Chadwick with husband, Edward T., Kimberlen, to her left, Bennie Allen, Franklin Jr, holding Franklin III. Standing are Stacy Chadwick, Winstona Chadwick, Ella Myers, me and Franklin Moss Sr., Erica Myers, Gretta Moss, Kenneth Moss, and Charles Myers. Back row left to right: Mia, Mr. Courtney Chadwick, Kevin Chadwick Jr., Mrs. Courtney Chadwick and her husband Kevin Chadwick Sr., and Donald L Chadwick. Sitting on the floor is Laila Chadwick, Kevin's daughter.

I always attended community events and supported students, parents, teachers, and school administrators. In front from left to right: Baldwin R. Brown, Willie B. Jones, me, Connor Brown, and Kena Brown. Back row: Dr. Eddie McAnthony, Keith Christmas, Lonnie Curley, Joe Scott, and Velois Curley.

One project I am proud of is the Rebranding of the East Fort Worth schools and the Stop Six neighborhood in FWISD. With the assistance of administration and staff, the Eastside Resource Center was born on the Sunrise Elementary Campus. The school district

My passion is volunteering at the Family Action Center FWISD resource center in east Fort Worth and distributing food at the church. From the left: Nakia Cole, coordinator, me, and Dr. Carlos Walker, director.

then assigned Dr. Carlos Walker, director, and Nakia Cole, assistant director, in 2016 to operate the center. Carlos and Nakia developed a relationship with the East Fort Worth neighborhoods and created opportunities to start the rebranding project. Their efforts continue to elevate students and the community. The two have supported the district's schools and provided support to families, including health care and social services to needy families.

As a newly elected school board trustee for District 3, I visited all the schools in the district I served. I noticed that many students in the schools located east of I-35 required assistance with reading or were reading below their grade level. These schools faced high teacher turnover, which hindered student learning because of a lack of resources, including certified teachers and teaching materials. I spoke with many teachers and students. I asked each person, "Tell me what you think would improve the student achievement in your school?" When I spoke to the parents, their concerns were the same: "Our schools lack adequate resources." As I left the high school, a teacher pulled me into the lounge and whispered, "Mrs. Moss, our principal is not certified; please check downtown."

After raising these concerns to the attention of the then-superintendent, Dr. Roberts, they initially dismissed my concerns as a mistake. However, they eventually realized the seriousness of the issues, and the superintendent confirmed that the high school's principal in District 3 required certification and that there had been an error in placement. The high school received a new principal, who played a role in addressing the issue of inadequate resources.

Dr. Thomas Tocco was superintendent of FWISD from 1994 to 2004. He focused on appointing the best administrators for various positions during his tenure. In 1995, Dr. Tocco launched the Elementary Schools Initiative to transform the lowest-performing schools in the district. The initiative offered the best teachers an attractive salary to teach in the underprivileged areas. By 1999, FWISD had no low-performing schools and 96 percent of students read on grade level. However, the district had a high drop-out rate.

In 2001, two school board members requested that Dr. Tocco stop allocating funds for the Elementary Schools Initiative in District 3. He discontinued the program, and after two years without funding, the schools in the area struggled with reading. To address the reading problem, Mr. Dansby and Dr. Tocco reviewed Houston ISD's reading program and approved the "Open Court" and "Reading Mastery" textbooks. They implemented the reading mastery program in the schools in District 3.

Dr. Tocco resigned in 2004 after a kickback scheme surfaced. Despite the controversy, board members praised him for increasing test scores and reducing the achievement gap between black, Hispanic, and Anglo students. Dr. Tocco made it mandatory for teachers to attend all workshops and learn how to implement the reading programs. (mfrazier@star-telegram.com)

In 2003, Mr. Joe Ross became superintendent of FWISD. He wanted something other than the interim superintendent title.

In 2005, Dr. Melody Johnson assumed the role of superintendent of FWISD. During her tenure, she dismantled the reading programs for students of color (Open Court and Reading Mastery), including the school curriculum. Her administration threw out the baby with the bath water and caused the school's academic ratings to plummet to the lowest between 2005 and 2011. Dr. Johnson abruptly resigned as superintendent in September 2011.

In 2012, Walter Dansby became the first African American Superintendent at FWISD after serving the district for 40 years. As he took on his new role, Dansby quickly identified that 27 schools in the district were performing poorly. He was the first to introduce Equity models to the administration and school board to tackle this issue. Unfortunately, some board members disagreed with his approach, and that led to his resignation in 2014. Despite this setback, he received nearly one million dollars in a compensation package over seven months. I wholeheartedly commend him for his unwavering commitment to educating students and his vision to provide resources to the students with the greatest need.

Thank you, Mr. Walter Dansby, the first African American elected as Superintendent of FWISD.

In 2015, Dr. Kent Paredes Scribner assumed the role of Superintendent at FWISD. Twenty-one schools in the district were academically low-performing. Over the years, Dr. Scribner focused on promoting racial equity and bridging the gaps in academic achievement. He worked with the school board to dismantle the systems that have historically reinforced these disparities. In 2022, Dr. Scribner resigned from his position as superintendent. During his tenure, the district received a B rating.

During my 29 years as a school board trustee for District 3, I visited all the schools I served, read to students during literacy week, and greeted graduating seniors at Paul Laurence Dunbar High School. I am grateful to Mrs. Willie B. Jones, former English teacher at Dunbar. I asked her to help me critique my speeches for 29 graduation ceremonies.

At my retirement celebration, I thanked the principals in FWISD, particularly those in District 3, for their tireless work and commitment to students. My retirement celebration in May 2019 came as a surprise. The gathering brought laughter, joy, and happiness. What a fantastic send-off! FWISD planned my retirement event at Christene Chadwick Moss Elementary School with the assistance of the principal, Mrs. Charla Staten, and staff. The Greater Fort Worth Area Negro Business and Professional Women's Club hosted the evening. The students from the elementary schools across the district were phenomenal and performed amazingly. Many of my constituents were in attendance, including Rev. Crane, the pastor of True Vine Baptist church across the street who adopted C.C. Moss in 2001; my minister, Rev. Bruce D. Datcher, and members from my church, school friends, community, and personal friends. Serving the school administrators, teachers, staff, students, and parents as the FWISD School Board Trustee was a fantastic journey.

I delivered encouraging words to the graduating seniors during their Graduating Exercises annually in May for 29 years. "Forget the sky. There's no limit to what you can achieve."

CHAPTER TWELVE

Bye, Bye Politics, Hello, Grandchildren

In past years I said, "Once I retire, I'll have more time to spend with my grandchildren."

But my children responded, "Mother, you will have more time to babysit your grandchildren."

The love and care I receive from my grandchildren is an incredibly emotional experience. I love the unique hugs and passionate kisses they give me. They bring so much joy to my everyday life. Our bond is strong. I have five grandchildren who are all outstanding members of my family. Their ages are 7, 13, 17, 36, and 38.

My daughter, Kim, had my first granddaughter, Kristen, in 1985, and my second granddaughter, Jorgette, was born in Germany in 1987. Edmond's daughter, Madeleine, was born in 2005. Franklin Jr. has two sons, Micah and Franklin III. My grandchildren are vocal, assertive and love asking for things. They send me a shopping list for their birthday or Christmas, and I usually buy them a gift card or ask for an Amazon link. We love to spoil our grandchildren but also love to send them home afterwards. I also have three great-grandchildren, Aaron Jr., Ayra, and Ahri.

In 2005, a significant event occurred in my granddaughter's life, Kristen Monea Simpson. The Ambassadors of Fort Worth, Inc., presented her at the Fort Worth Convention Center in downtown

Fort Worth. This momentous occasion celebrated Kristen and ten other young ladies 'debut into society. The Ambassadors recognized Kristen's outstanding achievements and sponsored her debut, emphasizing the significance of her accomplishments.

Kristen graduated from Pine Forest High School in Fayetteville, North Carolina. There, she served as the Captain of the Varsity cheerleaders 4A conference and was a Future Teachers of America member. She was also awarded the title of Most Talented Senior in 2003. She then attended Fayetteville State University, majoring in Psychology with a minor in English. She follows in the footsteps of her relatives, Drelesia Moss, Nichole Moss, and Charlotte Darden. The Fort Worth Assembly had presented my sister, Dr. Mossey Neloise Chadwick Haynes, and Kristen's mother, Kimberlen Camila Moss, in 1981.

In 2007, my second granddaughter, Jorgette Louise Simpson, debuted at the Fort Worth Convention Center in downtown Fort Worth as part of The Ambassadors' presentation. She was elegantly dressed in a formal white silk ball gown embellished with white lace, long-sleeved kid gloves, pearls, and all-white accessories.

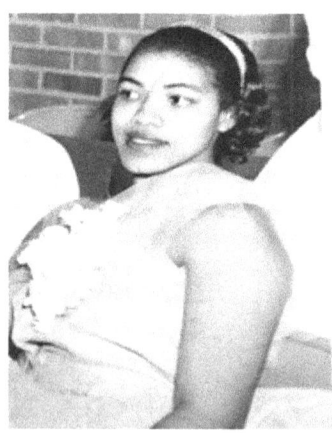

My sister, Mossey, was presented in 1954 by the Fort Worth Assembly. She was my second role model.

My son, Edmond, was presented in 1978 by Jack & Jill of America in the Beautillion Ball.

A ROSE AMONGST THE WEEDS 161

My daughter, Kimberlen, was presented in 1981 by the Fort Worth Assembly.

My son, Franklin Jr., was presented in 2000 by Jack & Jill of America Ball.

Frank and I, along with my sister-in-law, Winstona, and my brother, Adolphus, at the Ambassadors of Fort Worth Ball.

My granddaughter, Kristen Simpson was presented in 2005 by the Ambassadors of Fort Worth, Inc.,at the Fort Worth Convention Center BallRoom. Escort, her uncle Franklin Moss Jr.

My granddaughter, Jorgette Simpson, was presented in 2008 by the Ambassadors of Fort Worth. Escort, her uncle, Franklin Moss Jr.

One of my goals was to take my grandchildren to the White House. I contacted my friend, Congressman Marc Veasey, and requested a family tour of the White House. My granddaughter, Madeleine, and my grandson, Micah, were excited to check this off their bucket list. We took the trip seriously and planned it carefully with the Congressman's office for security reasons. I filled out all the forms and received our security passes from Congressman Veasey's office before the visit. We were thrilled when we boarded the plane to Washington, D.C., and even more excited when we arrived at the White House. We hoped to see the president walking across the lawn and waving to tourists.

While waiting in line to go on the White House tour, we saw Congressman Veasey. During the tour, I noticed that the First Lady had redecorated the rooms. The White House had a velvet rope along the tour route to prevent tourists from entering the rooms in the West Wing. Rich colors like blue, green, and red adorned each room's decor. The China room was the most stunning to me, with its beautiful patterns of fine china, tea sets, and decorations.

When I traveled to Washington D.C. for a workshop around 2001 and scheduled a White House tour for Franklin Jr. It was a chilly day, and we felt like our feet were freezing. The next day, it snowed. We had our security passes, so we did not have to wait in a long line. We toured for less than thirty minutes, and every room was like a picture book with colorful paintings on the walls. The line progressed from room to room. It was all so elegant. Franklin Jr. jokingly asked me what would happen if he sat in the big red chair, and I warned him not to touch anything lest the security men take him away. I added I couldn't afford to replace any furniture or teapots.

Opal Lee, my friend and Soror of Zeta Phi Beta Sorority, Psi Zeta Chapter, walked across America to raise awareness of the importance of freedom on June 19, commemorating enslaved people's emancipation in Texas. After elected officials and the

Dr. Opal Lee, "The Grandmother of Juneteenth," and I enjoying tea at the Como Community Center."

community marched yearly in Fort Worth with her, the bill to make June 19 a state holiday passed in 1979, and on June 17, 2021, it became a federal holiday. Mrs. Lee, now known as "The Grandmother of Juneteenth," had her portrait unveiled in the Texas State Senate Chambers on February 8, 2023, which made her the second black person to have a portrait hung in the Senate. The late Representative Barbara Jordan was the first.

CHAPTER THIRTEEN

Finally

I needed to believe that my past did not determine my present or future. To do so, I adopted a new mindset and acknowledged that with God, all things are possible (Luke 18:27). My mother taught me that even seemingly impossible goals can be achieved as we serve a God who created everything out of nothing (Hebrews 11:30). "Give him your 'nothingness' and watch him go to work." All he needs is our faith and belief in Him; He will do the rest.

My only living sibling is Donald L Chadwick, who is 72. Sadly, Edward Thomas Chadwick passed away while I was drafting my book on January 10, 2023, at 86 years old. My husband, Frank, is no longer an elected official. However, he still works as a realtor and is active in the community. My first-born son, Edmond Lorance Moss, has worked in the finance department at the Phi Beta Sigma headquarters in Washington, DC, for 11 years. My middle child, Kimberlen Camelia Moss Simpson, retired from nursing due to Lupus. She received an honorable discharge from the armed forces, and lives in Little Elm, Texas. My last-born son, Franklin Douglas Moss Jr., is the CEO of "Franklin & Anthony, Clothier," and is celebrating his anniversary. My daughter-in-law, Mia Moss, owns and operates a coffee boutique called Black Coffee in East Fort Worth. She recently celebrated her fifth anniversary.

After two divorces from the same man and having two children, I believed God would send me a suitable husband for myself and my children. I left a marriage that had become unhealthy for my family and found a place to go and someone to help care for my children. But I chose not to live with an unfaithful partner. Early life mistakes should not determine one's destiny or success. Circumstances forced me to leave school in the eleventh grade. Constantly, I reminded myself that dropping out did not define me and that I could still achieve my goals. God helped me by planting love and a forgiving spirit in my heart. He ordered my steps and gave me a positive vision for my life.

While showing gratitude to God for all the things He has done for me, I remembered, in late 1965, the close encounter I had with death. I was in my Volkswagen, driving like a bat out of hell to pick up my children, who were at my mother's house. I always followed the road around Como Lake. This time, it was slippery and wet from rain. My car slid off the road to the lake's edge as I hit the curve. When the car stopped, the front wheels were at the edge of the water line. I could feel my body going into shock. I said, "Save me, Jesus!" I could not move because I thought the car would slide into the lake.

A truck driver saw me slide off the road and stopped to help. The man said "Get out of the car!" I froze in place. He said, "If you don't get out of the car, the soft mud is going to take the car down to the bottom of the lake."

I could not back the car up; I was shaking badly. The driver helped me out of the car and backed the car back onto the road. He looked at me and asked, "Are you Tucker's girl?"

I said, "Yes, sir."

He told me to slow down around the lake, especially when it rains. He said, "We don't know how many cars are at the bottom of this lake!" I thanked the man, and thanked God. I promised I'd slow down. Never again did I take that scenic route around Como Lake. According to the news, in 2021, the city closed the lake entrance, constructed a fence around it, and dragged the lake during an environmental clean-up. The drag team found five cars and two bodies at the bottom of the lake.

Thank God I had a praying mother. I can still hear her praying as she kneeled at night, praying for her children, calling their names individually. Even today, I find myself following my mother's example. I pray for myself and my family, and I, too, call the names of my children out loud and individually: "Edmond," "Kim," and "Franklin Jr." That's because of my parents' upbringing through their morals, character, and values. I thank God for watching over me during my life's journey. My parents taught me a lot about God, but I learned how to live a Christian life and pray for myself. When I grew up and went into the world independently, I knew the difference between right and wrong.

Over the years, I have tried to be a role model for other young girls and women. We can create our destiny and be whatever we choose to be in life. Walk proud, walk with our heads up, and be unapologetic. Always give credit, respect, and recognition to individuals who help us. Be considerate of your parents for supporting us on the road to success.

Finally, I am happy that my influence extends beyond my retirement and will continue to live on in schools today. God has blessed me to live with my husband, Franklin Moss Sr., for 50 years in a community created and built by black families. I am not done yet.

My mantra is, "Integrity and education are two things that no one will ever be able to take away from you." It is all about our family and love for our family.

Lessons Learned From My Journey

1. Believe that God has a definite plan for your life.
2. Embrace struggles; they will make you stronger and more resilient.
3. Build strong relationships with your family and friends and cut off toxic people from your life.
4. Set ambitious goals and write them down with a clear action plan.
5. Consistently work towards your goals; do not let anything distract you.
6. Never give up on yourself; do not let anyone belittle your dreams.
7. If you need help, do not hesitate to ask someone who is trustworthy.
8. Be grateful for what others do for you, but also know your worth.
9. Accept that you are not perfect and are bound to make mistakes, but also learn from and grow from mistakes.
10. Give back, help those in need, and use your blessings to impact the world positively—volunteer for worthy causes.
11. Know that you do not have to scream at people to be effective. Thank God I was fortunate to inherit my mother's composure. I can stay calm while everything around me is falling apart.

The Accomplishments of Christene Chadwick Moss

I completed my education, became a registered nurse, and attained my master's degree. I served as an elected official as a school board trustee with Fort Worth ISD for twenty-nine years.

- A Lake Como-raised citizen, a long-term care nurse consultant, and a Fort Worth Public-School graduate. I hold an associate degree from Tarrant County Junior College, a long-term care administrator's license from El Centro College, and a license as a Registered Nurse. I hold a Bachelor of Science Degree in Sociology and Psychology from Texas Wesleyan College and a master's in Hospital Administration from Texas Woman's University. I served on the Fort Worth Independent School District Board of Trustees for 29 years. I taught at Tarrant County College as an adjunct professor.
- I am a strong advocate for all children and the "empowerment" of education. I am particularly passionate about literacy and FWISD's commitment to have all students reading on or above grade level by the time they are in second grade. As an elected school board trustee for 29 years, I passionately believe childhood literacy can determine future success in all subjects, including math and science. I've tirelessly worked to

remove barriers to learning and achievement while creating more access and opportunities for all students, especially black students.

- I have a strong calling for correcting social and racial injustices in the school district, therefore, I served as chairperson of the Racial Equity Committee of FWISD. Through my efforts, the committee established the FWISD racial equity policy with goals. The equity models are now part of the national conferences. This policy allowed the district to shift more resources to the schools with the most need, improving student outcomes for students of color. Additionally, I helped to get eligible high school seniors registered to vote and got the high school seniors in District 3 to the polls to vote.
- I've been involved with organizations over the years and have spent most of my life volunteering for organizations, and I will continue serving the people. With the assistance of FWISD, I established a Family Resource Center on the Sunrise – McMillan Elementary School campus. A ribbon-cutting ceremony did not occur during the 2019-2020 school year due to COVID-19. Every year, with the assistance of the principal and the students, I organize and lead the Dunbar Back-to-School Parade and Rally, focusing on students, parents, and community members to stress the importance of education and school attendance. I helped families connect with resources and school supplies at these events, setting them up for success in the school year ahead. We were always assured, as children, that we would one day amount to something. How can you give up with motivation like that?
- Former member of the National and Texas Caucus of the Black School Board Members and served as the state chair for the TCBSBM (2017-2018).

- Served as the co-chair of the education committees for the African American Leadership Institute and the Texas Wesleyan University Advisory Dual Credit Board.
- Member of Leadership Fort Worth and Forum Fort Worth since 1979.
- Hosted annual receptions for new teachers in District 3, welcoming them to FWISD and sharing historical information about the community and families they serve. I've honored longtime educators of excellence in the district, considered "legends," at a gala luncheon entitled Stop Six Legends of Education.
- Bus tours of the Stop-Six neighborhood are conducted each year for all new District 3 teachers, educating them about the history and legacy of Stop Six.
- Fellow for the Center for Reform of School Systems and served on the Council of the National Urban Board of Education Steering Committee (CUBE).
- Member of several organizations, including Zeta Phi Beta Sorority, Psi Zeta Chapter, Greater Fort Worth Area Negro Business and Professional Women's Club, Fort Worth Chapter Texas Coalition of black Democrats, and a life member of NAACP, Church Women United, and numerous other boards.
- Served on the boards of Women of Rotary, The Fort Worth Science and History, the Salvation Army, and Sickle Cell, to name a few.
- Received over 100 awards, honors, and recognitions for my contributions to education, volunteering, and community service, as well as from Congress.

Christene Chadwick Moss: Through the Years

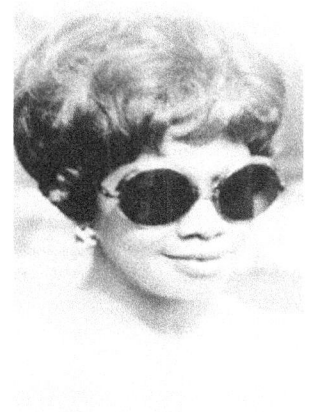

Me at age 18.   Me at age 29 when I dated Frank.

I thought I would spruce up in my 40s.

School board conferences across the country were part of the job.

I am the only living daughter of Dock Tucker and Lula Mae Chadwick.

My brother, Donald L and I are the only two siblings remaining in the Dock Tucker and Lula Mae Woods Chadwick family. Here, we celebrate my 80th birthday at Black Coffee Fort Worth.

Donald L is the only living son of Dock Tucker and Lula Mae Chadwick.

www.ingramcontent.com/pod-product-compliance
Lightning Source LLC
Chambersburg PA
CBHW061735070526
44585CB00024B/2683